# STONO

# STONO

Documenting and Interpreting
a Southern Slave Revolt

Edited by

MARK M. SMITH

University of South Carolina Press

© 2005 University of South Carolina

Published in Columbia, South Carolina,
by the University of South Carolina Press

Manufactured in the United States of America

14  13  12  11  10  09      10  9  8  7  6  5

Library of Congress Cataloging-in-Publication Data

Stono : documenting and interpreting a Southern slave revolt / edited by Mark M. Smith.
   p. cm.
   Includes bibliographical references and index.
   ISBN 1-57003-604-7 (cloth : alk. paper) — ISBN 1-57003-605-5 (pbk : alk. paper)
   1. Slave insurrections—South Carolina—Stono—History—18th century. 2. Slave
insurrections—South Carolina—Stono—History—18th century—Sources. 3. Stono
(S.C.)—Race relations—History—18th century. 4. Stono (S.C.)—Race relations—
History—18th century—Sources. 5. South Carolina—Race relations—History—18th
century. 6. South Carolina—Race relations—History—18th century—Sources. I. Smith,
Mark M. (Mark Michael), 1968– II. Title.
F279.S84S64 2005
975.7'9102—dc22

                                                                            2005016161

ISBN 13: 978-1-57003-605-7 (pbk)

Publication of this book is made possible in part by the generous support of the Partnership
Board of the Institute for Southern Studies at the University of South Carolina.

# CONTENTS

# Maps

# Acknowledgments

For his invaluable help and guidance on a variety of matters, I thank my colleague and friend Walter B. Edgar. Walter's counsel, his extraordinary knowledge of colonial South Carolina history, and his respect for the revealing detail has shaped this reader in some important ways. Robin Copp of the South Caroliniana Library rendered expert assistance with the maps, and Alex Moore proved not only a wonderful editor but also full of helpful advice. Thanks also go to my wife, Catherine, for her excellent detective work, to Mike Reynolds for his help in the archives, and to the undergraduate students who took my course the Historian's Craft in spring 2005 (particularly to Christopher Hulbert for alerting me to an otherwise unknown newspaper account). David Prior's help with the index was invaluable, as was Peter Coclanis's guidance and support for the project.

Peter Wood, John Thornton, and Ted Pearson were all immensely helpful when it came to securing permission to reprint the edited versions of their work. I remain in their debt.

This book has been published with the generous financial assistance of the Institute for Southern Studies at the University of South Carolina. I gratefully acknowledge this support.

# INTRODUCTION

## Finding Stono

Live oak branches braid high above, their bark fingers capillaries against blue sky just off U.S. Highway 17, about twenty miles southwest of Charleston, South Carolina. Grottolike, the trees lead to a plantation, "a short distance north of the road to Jacksonboro ferry," a place "called 'Battlefield.'"[1] Visible clues to the area's bloody history are few, nonexistent really. You'd never guess that hereabouts witnessed one of the largest and costliest slave revolts in colonial North America. Nothing suggests the beheadings, the wailing, the ferocity of battle that could be seen and heard during the Stono Rebellion in 1739.

Tourists rarely go to Stono, and even when they do, explaining the context, nature, meaning, and significance of the revolt is beyond the narrative and analytic powers of a snappy historical marker. Slave revolts are complicated things, and Stono is no exception.[2] The slaves involved in the Stono insurrection left few clues indicating why and how they revolted, and most of the evidence comes to us, often secondhand, from whites who themselves sometimes disagreed on important details. Even basic facts are annoyingly elusive. Who led the slaves, and what was his name? Was it Jemey/Jemmy, Arnold, Cato? How many slaves were involved in the revolt? How many died? How many whites were killed? When did the revolt start? Late on September 8? Or was it early on September 9? When did the rebellion end? Did it end quickly, as some contemporaries claimed, or did it last longer than just a few days?

Assessing the meaning and nature of the revolt is also difficult. At first blush Stono is impossibly contradictory, an event framed in binaries, seemingly irreconcilable opposites. The rebels were bloodthirsty and brutal yet rational and discriminating; they cut off white heads even as they used their minds; the revolt was intensely local and deeply connected to larger developments in the Atlantic world; the participants were at once Kongolese Africans and influenced by Portuguese Catholics; they fought as soldiers and prayed as Christians; some were loyal to their masters, others loyal to their cause; the event was timed precisely yet hobbled by chance. The list could go on. In some important respects though, the meaning of the Stono Rebellion, as the documents and essays presented in this collection show, is best understood not by trying to flatten the binaries but, rather, by treating them as reliable indicators of the complicated, textured, multivalent world in which the slaves and white South Carolinians lived in 1739.

The Stono Rebellion occurred in a decade noted for its slave unrest. As historian Edward A. Pearson notes (see essay 3 in this collection): "The 1730s was a decade of slave unrest throughout the New World plantation complex. Conspiracies were uncovered in the Bahamas in 1734 and in Antigua a year later, while war between colonists and maroons broke out on Jamaica in 1739." Other rebellions erupted on St. John in 1733 and on Guadalupe four years later. "Part of the Atlantic system, South Carolina likewise experienced unrest and discontent among its slave population as well as military threats from the Spanish." Enslaved people throughout the New World rejected bondage and either ran away to, or fought for, liberty. Sometimes, as at Stono, they did both at once. Regardless of their location, slave rebels used similar strategies and tactics to achieve their ends. They appropriated forms of punishment and violence whites used with slaves, such as beheading. In slave hands decapitation became a direct challenge to white authority, an inversion of customary power relations. Arson was also common both in the Caribbean and on the North American mainland as a means of destroying slaveholders' property (of property attacking property) and as a mechanism for alerting potential rebels to the act of insurrection. Did the slaves who conspired to revolt in New York City in 1741, those on the Danish island of St. John who revolted in 1733, those slaves and Irish workers who machinated to burn Savannah, Georgia, in 1738, and those who rebelled at Stono in 1739 act in concert, with knowledge of one another's revolts? Hardly. Communication networks, while more evolved among the dispossessed than we are sometimes apt to believe, were nonetheless too immature, too capricious to allow for that kind of coordination. Still the conspiracies and revolts of the period are, in the words of two recent historians, best "understood . . . by attending to the Atlantic experiences of the conspirators," by understanding the connections among "military regiments, the plantation, the waterfront gang, the religious conventicler, and the ethnic tribe or clan."[3] As the articles reprinted here suggest, the Stono Rebellion cannot be properly or fully understood without attention to this larger context. While the insurrection at Stono was not a conscious "challenge to the world capitalist system" of which it was part, it was nevertheless a product of that system and the revolt shaped its evolution. Even as many of the Stono slaves probably sought to escape and establish autonomy rather than initiate revolutionary upheaval, their actions were guided by transatlantic connections, and the revolt itself influenced not only the political, economic, and social future of South Carolina slaveholding society but also became part of a much larger imperial struggle between England and Spain over the southeastern part of North America.[4] After all it is worth remembering that a century before antebellum slaves looked north to freedom, they looked south to Spanish promises of liberty for those who escaped and reached Florida. Slaves in South Carolina had been running to northern Spanish Florida for years, and the Stono Rebellion continued the practice. The revolt was

both a mass act of escape and a genuine insurrection, replete with inte
implications. The War of Jenkins' Ear between England and Spain broke o
1739 and lasted until 1748, and South Carolinians' conviction that the Spanish had
been instrumental in fomenting the revolt led them to support an attack on Florida
mounted by Gen. James Oglethorpe in early 1740.[5]

The revolt itself began on Sunday, September 9, 1739, following a meeting on
the previous night. Early that morning the conspirators—precisely how many remains unclear—met at the Stono River in St. Paul's Parish. From there they moved
on to Stono Bridge and, having stolen guns from a local store, killed five whites,
burned a house, and continued southward. Before sunup the rebels reached a tavern. They spared the innkeeper—apparently the rebels understood him to be a kind
master—but they killed his neighbors and burned four of their houses. At this point
other slaves joined the rebellion, and the enlarged group continued south, banging
drums and holding aloft some sort of flag or banner.

By pure chance Lt. Gov. William Bull and four companions were on their way
back from Granville County, South Carolina, and they encountered the insurgents
at about eleven o'clock in the morning. According to Bull's account, by this point
the rebels had slain twenty-one whites and headed toward Georgia, killing and
burning as they went. Courtesy of their horses, Bull and his companions escaped
the rebels and alerted the militia and local planters. In the meantime the insurgents
continued southward. Between sixty and a hundred strong, they stopped in a field
—the battlefield—near Jacksonburough ferry. By this time it was late afternoon, and
the original group had covered about ten miles. Some were tired, others drunk. For
whatever reason they paused, deciding not to cross the Edisto River just yet. It was
at this point—around four o'clock—that Bull's men and the militia, about one hundred of them, caught up with the Stono rebels.

The rebels fought well and bravely, but the armed militia won the fight at the
battlefield. In the midst of battle about thirty insurgents escaped, many of whom
were hunted down in the days and weeks following. Planters released the slaves
they believed had been coerced to join the rebellion; those they considered willing
insurgents they shot. They decapitated a few of them and set their heads on posts
as a grisly warning.

Echoes of the revolt lingered. On the following Sunday militiamen encountered
a large group of disbanded rebels thirty miles south, where a second battle ensued.
Even though whites believed this fight ended the revolt, many remained cagey and
jittery. Militia companies were on guard, and a few planters, fearing that not all the
rebels had been rounded up, left the region. They were right to be concerned: one
leader was not captured until 1742.

White authorities dealt with the revolt in two ways. First, they rewarded slaves
who, in their estimation, had remained loyal to whites during the rebellion. In the

longer term, the rebellion led South Carolina authorities to introduce, according to one historian, "a fundamental alteration in the character of Carolina society, with a less open and compromising slave system." Specifically, the insurrection resulted in the 1740 Negro Act, which, among many other things, made patrol service mandatory for militiamen. In an attempt to slow the growth of South Carolina's majority black population, authorities also introduced a prohibitive duty on the importation of new slaves that went into effect in 1741. The duty doubled the price of slaves in an effort not only to limit the number of Africans in the colony but also to provide revenue to encourage the immigration of white European settlers. The measures weren't especially effective. Although few Africans were brought to South Carolina in the 1740s, just over fifty thousand came in between 1750 and the American Revolution. By 1775 almost 60 percent of South Carolina's population was black.[6]

Clearly, the Stono Rebellion resulted not only in closer surveillance of slaves but in increased responsibilities of masters that, ironically enough, imposed on their liberties. The legislation of 1740 took away an important right held by masters—the right to manumit slaves—and placed that authority in the hands of the state. The Stono revolt also had the effect of galvanizing white South Carolina society. Tensions with the Spanish, the challenge to stability and order posed by the Great Awakening, difficulties with Indians, and the events at Stono, according to historian Robert M. Weir, "combined to produce an unprecedented willingness on the part of local leaders to compromise and cooperate."[7] But white unity came with bloody price tag: all told, the revolt took about twenty white and forty black lives.

The relatively few public contemporary accounts of the Stono Rebellion—the newspapers in South Carolina were silent because whites feared that news of the revolt would only incite other rebellions—does not mean that the Stono insurrection isn't historically recoverable.[8] This reader presents all of the most important primary sources relating to the Stono Rebellion. Some of the documents are reprinted here for the first time (documents 14 and 15) and are largely unknown even to specialists in the field. In general the documents, each of which I've introduced and contextualized, help students understand contemporary views of the revolt and gauge its impact on colonial South Carolina society.

The relative dearth of primary evidence—especially regarding the slaves' motivation—hasn't hampered historians in writing about the Stono Rebellion. In fact the paucity has probably helped historians think imaginatively about the episode and encouraged them to pay keen attention to the kind of details often overlooked in better-documented revolts. The four essays presented here show how historians have used the documents to construct sometimes radically different interpretations of the revolt's cause, meaning, and effects.

The essays, by Peter H. Wood, John K. Thornton, Edward A. Pearson, as well as my own effort, by no means exhaust what has been written about the Stono insurrection.

Richard Cullen Rath's recent work, for example, has made imaginative connections linking drums, music, fighting style, and ethnicity in the revolt. Along similar lines Peter Charles Hoffer speculates creatively on the importance of sound and sight during the revolt.[9] But the remarks by Rath and Hoffer on Stono are brief compared to the fuller articles reprinted here. Moreover, the four pieces included in this collection show how historians build on one another's work in an effort to advance historical understanding, sometimes using the same sources differently, sometimes using newly discovered sources, and almost always engaging with and building on earlier interpretive insights and analyses. To help students understand how historians employ a variety of primary documents in the construction of their arguments and to illustrate how interpretations evolve historiographically, I have opted to retain the notes. They allow the reader to follow easily the historian's line of thinking and specific use of evidence.

Lastly, for the sake of convenience, I've constructed a working bibliography of primary and secondary sources on the Stono revolt. It does not pretend to be comprehensive, but it is a useful starting point for anyone beginning research on the topic.

## Notes

1. Henry A. M. Smith, "Willtown or New London," *South Carolina Historical and Genealogical Magazine* 10 (January 1909): 28. For helpful coverage of the revolt—as well as photographs of Battlefield plantation—see Roddie Burris, "Failed Uprising Resulted in Harsher Life for Slaves," *Columbia (S.C.) State*, February 2, 2003, p. B6.

2. The Stono River Slave Rebellion Site is on the National Register of Historic Places and was designated a National Historic Landmark in 1974. The historic marker, located in "Rantowles vicinity" on the north side of U.S. Highway 17 and the west bank of the Wallace River, reads in part: "On September 9–10, an Angolan slave named Jemmy led a slave rebellion involving some 80 slaves enlisted from plantation areas." It notes that the slaves were headed to St. Augustine, the encounter with the militia, and the effect of the rebellion on South Carolina's slave codes. The marker is most readily accessed in *African American Historic Places in South Carolina* (Columbia: South Carolina Department of Archives and History, State Historic Preservation Office, March 2005), pp. 16–17, available online at http://www.state.sc.us/scdah/aframsites.pdf.

3. On the importance of situating colonial slave revolts in an Atlantic context and on the role of arson, see Peter Linebaugh and Marcus Rediker, *The Many-Headed Hydra: Sailors, Slaves, Commoners, and the Hidden History of the Revolutionary Atlantic* (Boston: Beacon, 2000), pp. 174–98 (quotation on p. 179; the discussion of arson is on pp. 197–98). Of course, the question of whether or not slave revolts were rooted in the larger international revolutionary process has a deep genealogy. Start, most obviously, with Herbert Aptheker's *American Negro Slave Revolts* (1943; rept., New York: International Publishers, 1993); and C. L. R. James, *Black Jacobins: Toussaint L'Ouverture and the San Domingo Revolution* (New York: Dial, 1938). See also Eugene D. Genovese, "Herbert Aptheker's Achievement," in *In Resistance: Studies in African, Caribbean, and*

*Afro-American History,* ed. Gary Y. Okihiro (Amherst: University of Massachusetts Press, 1986), p. 23.

4. Genovese, *From Rebellion to Revolution: Afro-American Slave Revolts in the Making of the Modern World* (Baton Rouge: Louisiana State University Press, 1979), p. xxi. See also Marvin L. Michael Kay and Lorin Lee Cary, "'They Are Indeed the Constant Plague of Their Tyrants': Slave Defence of a Moral Economy in Colonial North Carolina, 1748–1772," in *Out of the House of Bondage: Runaways, Resistance, and Marronage in Africa and the New World,* ed. Gad Heuman (London: Cass, 1986), p. 40.

5. Robert M. Weir, *Colonial South Carolina: A History* (Millwood, N.Y.: KTO, 1983), pp. 117–18. See also John J. TePaske, "The Fugitive Slave: Intercolonial Rivalry and Spanish Slave Policy, 1687–1764," in *Eighteenth-Century Florida and Its Borderlands,* ed. Samuel Proctor, pp. 1–12 (Gainesville: University Presses of Florida, 1975). For earlier instances of slaves running away to St. Augustine and the "Primus" slave plot of 1720, see John Alexander Moore, "Royalizing South Carolina: The Revolution of 1719 and the Evolution of Early South Carolina Government" (Ph.D. diss., University of South Carolina, 1991), pp. 375–79. On the revolt's overtly military and masculine qualities, see Elizabeth Fox-Genovese, "Strategies and Forms of Resistance," in *In Resistance,* ed. Okihiro, pp. 151–52.

6. Darold D. Wax, "'The Great Risque We Run': The Aftermath of Slave Rebellion at Stono, South Carolina, 1739–1745," *Journal of Negro History* 67 (Summer 1982): 136–47 (quotation on p. 138); numbers are in Walter B. Edgar, *South Carolina: A History* (Columbia: University of South Carolina Press, 1998), pp. 77–78.

7. Weir, *Colonial South Carolina,* p. 124. See also Robert Olwell, *Masters, Slaves, and Subjects: The Culture of Power in the South Carolina Low Country, 1740–1790* (Ithaca, N.Y.: Cornell University Press, 1998), esp. pp. 35–36.

8. See Burris, "Failed Uprising," p. B6. On page 333 of his 1779 historical account of the revolt (see document 13), Alexander Hewatt offers the following footnote: "A very full account of this insurrection is to be found in the Carolina Gazette, in the Charlestown library." I have yet to find this account. As the *Carolina Gazette* (printed by Freneau and Paine) was first published in 1798, Hewatt probably meant the *South-Carolina Gazette,* which began publication in 1732. If so, the absence of a date in Hewatt's reference means that the account—if it has survived—was not necessarily published in 1739. Conceivably, it could have appeared anytime after the revolt (perhaps as a retrospective) and before the late 1770s, when Hewatt wrote his history. Descriptions of the revolt did appear in other newspapers, however. The account published in the November 1–8 issue of the *Boston Weekly News-Letter* (reprinted as document 5) was the most detailed but not the first. The weekly *Boston Gazette,* based on "Letters from Charlestown in South Carolina, of the 14th of September," offered the following description in its October 29–November 5, 1739, issue on page 2: "about 100 rebellious Negroes got together, arm'd, and murder'd twenty one white Persons, Men, Women and Children, in a most barbarous Manner, which put the whole Country into the utmost Confusion, expecting it a general Plot thro' the whole Province, but it does not yet appear that it was ever laid deeper than for the Nation of *Angolas.* The Negroes were immediately pursu'd, thirty of them kill'd, several taken, and the rest put to the Rout."

9. Richard Cullen Rath, *How Early America Sounded* (Ithaca, N.Y.: Cornell University Press, 2003), pp. 46–89; Rath, "Drums and Power: Ways of Creolizing Music in Coastal South Carolina

and Georgia, 1730–90," in *Creolization in the Americas,* ed. David Buisseret and Steven G. Reinhardt, pp. 99–130 (College Station: Texas A&M University Press, 2000); Peter Charles Hoffer, *Sensory Worlds in Early America* (Baltimore: Johns Hopkins University Press, 2003), pp. 151–59. Parts of Hoffer's account of the revolt are entertainingly but wildly speculative. For example, there is no way Hoffer could know that the rebels "swore a blood oath to stand, march, and fight as one" (p. 152). Not only does the evidence suggest that they didn't fight as one, but Hoffer offers no documentation to support this claim.

# I. Documenting Stono

The following documents are presented in rough chronological order, beginning with those sources recorded nearest in time to the rebellion. The sources span about two centuries: the first and earliest is dated September 13, 1739; the last was recorded in the 1930s. While not all the sources agree on all points, together they allow the historian to reconstruct key features of the Stono Rebellion. Several questions should accompany a close reading of each source: On which points do these primary source documents agree and disagree? Which sources are most reliable and why? What seems fanciful, and what are the possible sources of bias?

Document 1

# SPANISH DESIGNS AND SLAVE RESISTANCE

The following accounts, written just before and after the revolt, are by Col. William Stephens. Stephens was something of a sentinel for the Trustees of colonial Georgia. He was sent to Savannah in 1737 to gather and offer the Trustees reliable, accurate information on the progress and condition of the colony. As such, Stephens kept detailed records. For the historian of the Stono Rebellion, two of his journal entries are especially important. The first entry, made six or so weeks before the revolt, suggests the role of the Spanish in fomenting the revolt and slave unrest generally; the second, written just a few days after the revolt, offers additional details concerning the revolt itself. On the whole Stephens's journal suggests that colonial slaveholding society was a nervous place, one where "spies" flourished, where one had to read faces and coloring carefully to verify or dispute claims, where strangers drew suspicious glances from authorities anxious about the safety of their slave-based society. Compare the details offered in this account to those offered in the other documents.

———•+•+•———

Sunday [July 29, 1739].   The ordinary Service of the Day was regularly observed. In the Evening, upon Intelligence, that a Person had been skulking in Town [Savannah], under the Character of a Jew practicing Surgery and Physick, ever since Friday; and giving out, that he came from North-Carolina, intending to go for Frederica, and hoped to get Leave to settle there; it was thought proper to have him taken up, and examined before the Magistrates; which was done: And it appeared by the Testimony of our principal Jews here, that he was not of that Religion: Then, upon asking him what Country he was of, he said, of Germany: But his Complexion not agreeing with that Climate, we could not presently give Credit to it: And moreover it appearing he had his Pockets well stored, and that finding he began to be suspected, he had agreed with some Hands to row him up the River in the Night to some convenient Place, from whence he might travel by Land as far South as Darien; we were more and more confirmed in our Opinions, that he was a dangerous

Source: "The Journal of William Stephens," in *The Colonial Records of the State of Georgia,* vol. 4, *Stephens' Journal 1737–1740,* ed. Allen D. Candler (Atlanta: Franklin, 1906), pp. 378–79, 412–13.

Person: whereupon it was thought needful to have his Pockets well searched, where he had Abundance of Papers, &c. among which, though we could not make a plain Discovery of his Designs, yet many Tokens appeared of his deserving to be taken good Care of: When he found that it was in vain for him to deny, what we could quickly prove, he confessed himself born in Old Spain; that he had been rambling for a few Years past, farther Northward, in the Practice of his Profession, particularly in Virginia and North-Carolina, &c. but had made no Abode in South-Carolina, nor seen Charles-Town for a long while past: But upon looking into his Papers, was evident he was in Charles-Town about a Fortnight or three Weeks since; which, as near as we could guess, was much about the Time that the Spanish Launch was lately there: It was plain that he had gone by several Names; and in short there was sufficient Reason for suspecting strongly that he was no better than a Spy: Whereupon he was committed to the Guard, to be there secured till the next convenient Opportunity of enquiring farther, after having made as strict an Examination as we could till Midnight. . . .

[Thursday, September 13, 1739.]   Towards Noon an Express arrived, with Letters of the 10th, from the Government at Charles-Town; and of Yesterday's Date from the Magistrates in and near Port-Royal, confirming the War [between England and Spain] being actually declared, which they had Advice of by a Sloop also from Rhode-Island, that arrived since the other which brought the first News of it: . . . in the Midst of these Hostilities from abroad, it was now their great Unhappiness to have a more dangerous Enemy in the Heart of their Country to deal with: For their Negroes had made an Insurrection, which began first at Stonoe (Midway between Charles-Town and Port-Royal) where they had forced a large Store, furnished themselves with Arms and Ammunition, killed all the Family on that Plantation, and divers other white People, burning and destroying all that came in their Way; so that the Messenger who came, told us the Country thereabout was full of Flames: Our Letters also informed us, that they were fearful lest it should prove general; and that the Militia was raised upon them throughout the whole Province; a Party of whom, of about twenty, had met and engaged ninety of them in one Body, of whom they had taken four Prisoners, and killed ten, &c. They farther wrote us, they had Reason to believe, that many of them would bend their Course to the South, and endeavour to cross the Savannah River; from whence they intended to go on for Augustin to the Spaniards: Wherefore they hoped we would do what we could, in securing the Passes on that River, promising a Reward of 50 *l.* Currency for every Negro taken alive, and delivered at Charles-Town; and 25 *l.* ditto for every one killed. Upon these Advices, we dispatched Intelligence of it to the Major, commanding in the South, who possibly might, by small Parties, intercept some of them, if they escaped in crossing the River Savannah, and pursued their March to the Southward

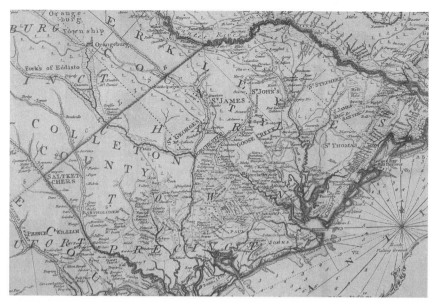

Detail of South Carolina lowcountry parishes. From James Cook, *A Map of the Province of South Carolina . . .* (London: Published according to Act of Parliament, 1773). Courtesy of the South Caroliniana Library, University of South Carolina.

Detail of the Ashley River and Stono River area. From James Cook, *A Map of the Province of South Carolina . . .* (London: Published according to Act of Parliament, 1773). Courtesy of the South Caroliniana Library, University of South Carolina.

by Land: And as we could ill spare any of the few Men we had, that were fit to bear Arms, and by so doing leave ourselves more and more defenceless, we sent immediately Notice of it to Mr. Montaigut, whose Plantation with Negroes is not many Miles distant, and who is also a military Officer himself; recommending it to him, to have a Guard at those Passes beyond him, and send proper Caution to the Fort at Palachocolas, farther than which would be needless: And we would do the best we could below, to the Mouth of the River. ———Now it fully appeared, that the securing that Spaniard some Time ago (*vide* July 29.) was not upon a groundless Suspicion (as some People then termed it, who are rarely pleased with whatever is done, because they have not the doing it) for it is more than probable, that he had been employed a pretty while, in corrupting the Negroes of Carolina; and was certainly with Don Pedro at Charles-Town, at the Time when he lately came thither with his Launch.

Document 2

# A Ranger Details the Insurrection

The following excerpt is from "A Ranger's Report of Travels with General Oglethorpe, 1739–1742," in which the author details when he first heard news of the revolt, what his party was told of the rebels' behavior, the numbers involved, and why the revolt failed. Throughout the summer of 1739 Gen. James Edward Oglethorpe (1696–1785)—commander in chief of the southern frontier and widely considered Georgia's first governor—was busily attempting to shore up alliances with a variety of southern Indian tribes and frustrate Spanish efforts to undermine Anglo-Indian relations on the southern frontier. We join Oglethorpe on his way back from a series of negotiations. The ranger refers to "this fort"—the trading post of Fort Augusta (where present-day Augusta sits)—and he makes reference to the Swiss settlement of Purysburg, about twenty miles outside Savannah.

<hr>

<u>Septr. 17th</u> [1739].   We set out from this Fort and as we were going down the River we met a Trading Boat going to Fort Augusta, the People on board her told us the Negroes in Carolina had raised up in Arms and killed about forty White People. We went to Fort Prince George where we found thirty men come from Purysburg to Strengthen the Fort. <u>Septr. 20th.</u> A Negroe came to the General and told him that what was said of the Negroes Rising in Carolina was True and that they had marched to Stono Bridge where they had Murthered two Storekeepers Cut their Heads off and Set them on the Stairs Robbed the stores of what they wanted and went on killing what Men, Women, and Children they met, Burning of Houses and Committing other Outrages, and that One hundred Planters who had assembled themselves together pursued them and found them in an open Field where they were Dancing being most of them drunk with the Liquors they found in the Stores, As soon as they saw their Masters they all made off as fast as they Could to a Thicket of Woods excepting One Negroe fellow who came up to his Master his Master asked him if he wanted to kill him the Negroe answered he did at the same time Snapping

Source: "A Ranger's Report of Travels with General Oglethorpe, 1739–1742," in *Travels in the American Colonies*, ed. Newton D. Mereness (New York: Macmillan, 1916), pp. 222–23.

a Pistoll at him but it mist fire and his Master shot him thro' the Head about fifty of these Villains attempted to go home but were taken by the Planters who Cutt off their heads and set them up at every Mile Post they came to.

Document 3

# NEWS OF THE REVOLT ENTERS
# PRIVATE CORRESPONDENCE

Robert Pringle (1702–1776) came to Charleston from Scotland in 1725. A factor for several English and American firms, Pringle made his money trading dry goods and, increasingly, rice. By the time he wrote the following letter, Pringle was well on his way to becoming an established, affluent, and respected member of Charleston society. In his letter to John Richards—with whom he did business in London—Pringle gives us the context for the revolt and refers to not only difficulties with the Spanish but also illness. Plainly, this was a worrying time for white South Carolinians, especially those with a political and economic stake in what was among British North America's most affluent and flourishing colonies. The revolt was sufficiently perturbing to have made its way into Pringle's private business correspondence.

———◆•◆•◆———

About Ten days agoe arriv'd here Via Boston, His Majestys Ship the *Tartar Pink*, Capt. George Townshend, Commander with Instructions for our Governour to grant Letters of Marque & Reprisal to any Vessells that have a mind to goe a Privateering on the Spaniards & all his Majestys Ships on the American Stations have Rendevous'd here in Order to goe a Cruizing on the Spaniards So that we may expect soon to see some Prizes brought in here.

I hope our Government will order Effectual methods for the taking of St. Augustine from the Spaniards which is now become a great Detriment to this Province by the Encouragement & Protection given by them to our Negroes that Run away there. An Insurrection has been made of late here in the Country by some Negroes in order to their Going there & in less than Twenty four hours they murthered in their way there between Twenty & Thirty white People & Burnt Severall houses before they were overtaken, tho' now most of the Gang are already taken or Cut to Peices [*sic*]. This has happened within these Three Weeks Past.

Source: Robert Pringle, Charles Town, to John Richards, London, 26 September, 1739, in *The Letterbook of Robert Pringle*, vol. 1, *April 2, 1737–September 25, 1742*, ed. Walter B. Edgar (Columbia: University of South Carolina Press, 1972), p. 135.

We have been Afflicted in this Town for these Two Months past with a great Sickness & Mortality by a Malignant Fever, which has Carried off a great many People, but as the Season comes in now Pretty Cool, hope will be more healthfull & that it will Please God to put a Stop to it.

Document 4

# OVERWORK AND RETALIATION?

This brief account, from a "Daily Register" (diary), was written by Johann Martin Boltzius (possibly with help from Israel Christian Gronau, his assistant). Both men were Lutheran ministers to the Salzburger community in Georgia. The Salzburgers were a group of about two hundred German Protestants who had been exiled from Salzburg in 1731 and who founded the town of Ebenezer in the religiously tolerant colony. Like James Oglethorpe (see document 2), the Salzburgers opposed the institution of slavery (Georgia did not permit it until 1749). The author notes that some rebels had made it to Georgia by September 26 (thus suggesting that the temporal and spatial parameters of the revolt were rather more elastic than is sometimes assumed) and establishes a possible connection between overwork and the revolt (see also document 12). *Jus talionis* refers to the right of retaliation.

———◆◆◆◆———

[Friday, September 28, 1739.]   A man brought the news that the Negroes or Moorish slaves are not yet pacified but are roaming around in gangs in the Carolina forests and that ten of them had come as far as the border of this country just two days ago. In answer to the request of the inhabitants of Savannah to use Moorish slaves for their work, the Lord Trustees have given the simple negative answer that they will never permit a single Black to come into the country, for which they have sufficient grounds that aim at the happiness of the subjects. Mr. Oglethorpe told us here that the misfortune with the Negro rebellion had begun on the day of the Lord, which these slaves must desecrate with work and in other ways at the desire, command, and compulsion of their masters and that we could recognize a *jus talionis* in it. I, however, ponder the fact that the mill in Old Ebenezer was also ruined by a flood on Sunday and that the work that was done then through necessity by the servants did no good.

Source: *Detailed Reports on the Salzburger Emigrants Who Settled in America . . . Edited by Samuel Urlsperger*, vol. 6, *1739*, trans. and ed. George Fenwick Jones and Renate Wilson (Athens: University of Georgia Press, 1981), p. 226. Title now published by and used with permission of Picton Press of Camden, Maine.

Document 5

# THE STONO REBELLION AS NATIONAL NEWS

By November news of the revolt was national. The *Boston Gazette* published a brief description in its October 29–November 5 issue (see note 8 of the editor's introduction). The following, "A Letter from South Carolina [September 28, 1739]," offered a fuller description and appeared in the November 1–8 issue of the *Boston Weekly News-Letter*. The unknown author describes the ending of the revolt by whites. Judging by other sources, was the white response as efficient, quick, and effective as the author suggests?

——◆◆◆◆——

About three Weeks past we had an Insurrection of our Negroes, who in one Night cut off about 25 Whites, and then form'd a considerable Body, burnt about 6 Houses, and sacrificed every Thing in their Way. We were immediately alarm'd, and under Arms; and the first Method we took was to secure our Ferries and Passes by Guards; and to send out a Body upon the Scout, which came up with them, and engag'd them. They gave two Fires, but without any Damage. We return'd the Fire, and bro't down 14 on the Spot; and pursuing after them, within two Days kill'd twenty odd more, some hang'd, and some Gibbeted alive. A Number came in and were seized and discharged; and some are yet out, but we hope will soon be taken. . . .

Document 6

# "Account of the Negroe Insurrection in South Carolina"

It is unclear who penned this account. Peter Wood in his essay gives James Oglethorpe as the author (see note 9 of Wood's essay), but other historians are less certain (see Herbert Aptheker, *American Negro Slave Revolts* [1943; rept., New York: International Publishers, 1993], p. 187, n. 73), and the source itself gives no clear indication. It appears to have been written in early October 1739. Despite the account's uncertain provenance, it contains details of great use to the historian. The account situates the revolt in the context of imperial tensions being played out on the colonial southeast, and the author sees the rebellion as part and parcel of a long-standing effort on the part of the Spanish to undermine the British presence in Georgia and South Carolina. The account also offers important details: it names the revolt's leader, identifies several whites by name, claims the slaves were Angolan, and depicts the rebels as thoughtful if violent men who killed some whites and spared others. The account refers to the "Saltzburghers," the same exiled Protestants noted in document 4. This account was reprinted in London's *Gentleman's Magazine* in March 1740 (see "Extract of a Letter from S. Carolina, dated October 2," vol. 10, pp. 127–29). What image does the account paint of the planters who suppressed the insurrection, and how does it compare with the depiction offered in other documents? According to this document, how long did the revolt last, and what numbers were involved?

———◆◆◆◆———

Sometime since there was a Proclamation published at Augustine, in which the King of Spain (then at Peace with Great Britain) promised Protection and Freedom to all Negroes [*sic*] Slaves that would resort thither. Certain Negroes belonging to Captain Davis escaped to Augustine, and were received there. They were demanded

Source: "An Account of the Negroe Insurrection in South Carolina," in *The Colonial Records of the State of Georgia*, ed. Allen D. Candler, Wm. L. Northern, and Lucian L. Knight (Atlanta: Byrd, 1913), vol. 22, pt. 2, pp. 232–36.

by General Oglethorpe who sent Lieutenant Demere to Augustine, and the Governour assured the General of his sincere Friendship, but at the same time showed his Orders from the Court of Spain, by which he was to receive all Run away Negroes. Of this other Negroes having notice, as it is believed, from the Spanish Emissaries, four or five who were Cattel-Hunters, and knew the Woods, some of whom belonged to Captain MacPherson, ran away with His Horses, wounded his Son and killed another Man. These marched f [sic] for Georgia, and were pursued, but the Rangers being then newly reduced [sic] the Countrey people could not overtake them, though they were discovered by the Saltzburghers, as they passed by Ebenezer. They reached Augustine, one only being killed and another wounded by the Indians in their flight. They were received there with great honours, one of them had a Commission given to him, and a Coat faced with Velvet. Amongst the Negroe Slaves there are a people brought from the Kingdom of Angola in Africa, many of these speak Portugueze (which Language is as near Spanish as Scotch is to English,) by reason that the Portugueze have considerable Settlement, and the Jesuits have a Mission and School in that Kingdom and many Thousands of the Negroes there profess the Roman Catholic Religion. Several Spaniards upon diverse Pretences have for some time past been strolling about Carolina, two of them, who will give no account of themselves have been taken up and committed to Jayl in Georgia. The good reception of the Negroes at Augustine was spread about, Several attempted to escape to the Spaniards, & were taken, one of them was hanged at Charles Town. In the latter end of July last Don Pedro, Colonel of the Spanish Horse, went in a Launch to Charles Town under pretence of a message to General Oglethorpe and the Lieutenant Governor.

On the 9th. day of September last being Sunday which is the day the Planters allow them to work for themselves, Some Angola Negroes assembled, to the number of Twenty; and one who was called Jemmy was their Captain, they suprized a Warehouse belonging to Mr. Hutchenson at a place called Stonehow [sic]; they there killed Mr. Robert Bathurst, and Mr. Gibbs, plundered the House and took a pretty many small Arms and Powder, which were there for Sale. Next they plundered and burnt Mr. Godfrey's house, and killed him, his Daughter and Son. They then turned back and marched Southward along Pons Pons, which is the Road through Georgia to Augustine, they passed Mr. Wallace's Taxern [sic] towards day break, and said they would not hurt him, for he was a good Man and kind to his Slaves, but they broke open and plundered Mr. Lemy's House, and killed him, his wife and Child. They marched on towards Mr. Rose's resolving to kill him; but he was saved by a Negroe, who having hid him went out and pacified the others. Several Negroes joined them, they calling out Liberty, marched on with Colours displayed, and two Drums beating, pursuing all the white people they met with, and killing Man Woman and Child when they could come up to them. Collonel Bull

Lieutenant Governour of South Carolina, who was then riding along the Road, discovered them, was pursued, and with much difficulty escaped & raised the Countrey. They burnt Colonel Hext's house and killed his Overseer and his Wife. They then burnt Mr. Sprye's house, then Mr. Sacheverell's, and then Mr. Nash's house, all lying upon the Pons Pons Road, and killed all the white People they found in them. Mr. Bullock got off, but they burnt his House, by this time many of them were drunk with the Rum they had taken in the Houses. They increased every minute by new Negroes coming to them, so that they were above Sixty, some say a hundred, on which they halted in a field, and set to dancing, Singing and beating Drums, to draw more Negroes to them, thinking they were now victorious over the whole Province, having marched ten miles & burnt all before them without Opposition, but the Militia being raised, the Planters with great briskness pursued them and when they came up, dismounting; charged them on foot. The Negroes were soon routed, though they behaved boldly several being killed on the Spot, many ran back to their Plantations thinking they had not been missed, but they were there taken and Shot, Such as were taken in the field also, were after being examined, shot on the Spot; and this is to be said to the honour of the Carolina Planters, that notwithstanding the Provocation they had received from so many Murders, they did not torture one Negroe, but only put them to an easy death. All that proved to be forced & were not concerned in the Murders & Burnings were pardoned, And this sudden Courage in the field, & the Humanity afterwards hath had so good an Effect that there hath been no farther Attempt, and the very Spirit of Revolt seems over. About 30 escaped from the fight, of which ten marched about 30 miles Southward, and being overtaken by the Planters on horseback, fought stoutly for some time and were all killed on the Spot. The rest are yet untaken. In the whole action about 40 Negroes and 20 whites were killed. The Lieutenant Governour sent an account of this to General Oglethorpe, who met the advices [sic] on his return from the Indian Nation[.] He immediately ordered a Troop of Rangers to be ranged, to patrole through Georgia, placed some Men in the Garrison at Palichocolas, which was before abandoned, and near which the Negroes formerly passed, being the only place where Horses can come to swim over the River Savannah for near 100 miles, ordered out the Indians in pursuit, and a Detachment of the Garrison at Port Royal to assist the Planters on any Occasion, and published a Proclamation ordering all the Constables &ca. of Georgia to pursue and seize all Negroes, with a Reward for any that should be taken. It is hoped these measures will prevent any Negroes from getting down to the Spaniards.

Document 7

# LIEUTENANT GOVERNOR BULL'S EYEWITNESS ACCOUNT

This document is the only firsthand account of the rebellion. Its author was William Bull (1683–1755), who encountered the Stono rebels on his way back from Granville County. As president of the Royal Council, Bull became acting governor of South Carolina on November 22, 1737, with the death of the lieutenant (and acting) governor, Thomas Broughton. Thanks to the support of his friend James Oglethorpe (see document 2), Bull was commissioned as lieutenant governor of the colony on June 3, 1738, and he continued in that position until the arrival of Gov. James Glen in December 1743 (for further details see the entry for Bull in *Biographical Directory of the South Carolina House of Representatives,* vol. 2, *The Commons House of Assembly, 1692–1775,* ed. Walter B. Edgar and N. Louise Bailey, pp. 120–22 [Columbia: University of South Carolina Press, 1997]). In Bull's estimation the Stono revolt was notable less because it was attempted and more because it was prevented. Apparently, slave escapes to Florida had become common by the time of the revolt. Bull's account also offers the historian extraordinary detail, explains the imperial and military significance of the revolt, and concludes with a useful section on measures taken to deal with the rebels and quash future insurrections.

My Lords,

I beg leave to lay before your Lordships an Account of our Affairs; first in regard to the Desertion of Our Negroes, who are encouraged to it by a Certain Proclamation published by the King of Spain's Order at St. Augustine declaring Freedom to all Negroes who should desert thither from the British Colonies; Since which Several parties have deserted and are there openly received and protected, many

Source: Lt. Gov. Sir William Bull to the Board of Trade, Charleston, October 5, 1739, (Received December 10, 1739), Sainsbury Transcripts, Records in the British Public Record Office Relating to South Carolina, 1711–1782, vol. 20, pp. 179–80, in the South Carolina Department of Archives and History, Columbia, S.C. (C.O. Papers, S.C. Original Correspondence, Secretary of State, 1730–1746, no. 5/388).

attempts of others have been discovered and prevented, notwithstanding which on the 9th of September last at Night a great number of Negroes Arose in Rebellion, broke open a Store where they got Arms, killed twenty one White Persons, and were marching the next morning in a Daring manner out of the Province, killing all they met, and burning Several Houses as they passed along the Road. I was returning from Granville County with four Gentlemen and met these rebels at Eleven a Clock in the forenoon, and fortunately deserned the approaching Danger time enough to avoid it, and to give notice to the Militia who on that Occasion behaved with so much expedition and bravery, as by four a Clock the Same day to come up with them and killed and took so many as put a stop to any further mischief at that time, forty four of them have been killed and Executed some few yet remain concealed in the Woods expecting the same Fate, seem desparate. If Such an attempt is made in a time of peace what might be expected if an Enemy Should appear upon our Frontier with a design to Invade us? which we have great reason to expect upon the first Notice of a Rupture, being fully informed by Several hands of the great Preparations made Sometime ago at the Havana, which according to late accounts lye ready waiting only for Orders to put that Design in Execution.

It was the Opinion of His Majesty's Council with several other Gentlemen that one of the most Effectual means that could be used at present to prevent such desertion of our Negroes, is to encourage some Indians by a suitable Reward to pursue and if possible to bring back the Deserters, and while the Indians are thus Employed they would be in the way ready to intercept others that might attempt to follow, and I have sent for the Chiefs of the Chickasaws living at New Windsor and the Catawbaw Indians for that purpose. . . .

Document 8

# Rewarding Indians, Catching Rebels

This document, part of a Commons House of Assembly Committee report read in late November 1739, elaborates on the use of Indians to catch slave rebels and betray plots and shows the lengths that planters and slaveholders went to disrupt plots in the immediate aftermath of Stono.

———◆◆◆◆◆———

1. ... your Committee find that a negro man named July belonging to Mr. Thomas Elliott was very early & chiefly instrumental in saving his Master & his Family from being destroyed by the Rebellious Negroes and that the Negro man July had at several times bravely fought against the Rebels and killed one of them. Your Committee therefore recommend that the Sd Negro July (as a reward for his faithful Services and for an Encouragement to other Slaves to follow his Example in case of the like Nature) shall have his Freedom and a Present of a Suit of Cloaths, Shirt, Hat, a pair of stockings and a pair of Shoes. . . .

5. That a Negro Man belonging to Mr John Smith named Quash did endeavour to take one of the Rebellious Negroes for which your Committee are of opinion that he should be rewarded with the sum of £10 in Cash.

6. That the Cloaths (herein before recommended by your Committee) to be given to the Slaves (as a Reward for their Fidelity) be made with blue Strouds faced up with Red & trimmed with brass Buttons.

7. That several of the Neighbouring Indians did assist in hunting for, taking and destroying the sd Rebellious Negroes, For which your Committee propose that the sd Indians be severally rewarded with a Coat, a Flap, a Hat, a pair of Indian Stockings, a Gun, 2 Pounds of Powder & 8 Pounds of Bullets, Which Indians Names are as follows (that is to say) Tobb, Old Jack, Peter, Tom and Philip and five other Indians (whose names your Committee do not know) that came down to Stono with Captain Coachman. . . .

Source: A Commons House of Assembly Committee Report, in a Message to the Governor's Council, *Journal of the Upper House*, no. 7 (November 29, 1739), pp. 266–67, South Carolina Department of Archives and History, Columbia, S.C.

Document 9

# Deserting Stono

Andrew Leslie was parson to St. Paul Parish. In this brief excerpt he suggests that small bands of Stono rebels roamed the vicinity for months after the revolt and kept whites on edge. Leslie has some details wrong, probably because he appears to have been recalling events almost four months old. For example, he incorrectly dates the revolt September 16. How else does this account depart from the others?

———◆•◆•◆———

An Insurrection of ye Negroes happened in my Parish Sept 16, who murdered 22 of my Parishioners in a most barbarous manner. Our militia came up [the?] next day about 4 in ye afternoon after a short engagement . . . ye rebels were so entirely defeated & dispersed yt there never were Seen above 6 or 7 together since. However several of my principal Parishioners, being apprehensive of Danger from ye Rebels Still outstanding carried their Families to Town for Safety, & if y Humour of moving continues a little longer, I shall have but a Small Congregation at Church.

Source: Andrew Leslie to the Society for the Propagation of the Gospel, January 7, 1739/40, Society for the Propagation of the Gospel Record, microfilm, reel 5, pp. 19–20, South Carolina Department of Archives and History, Columbia, S.C.

Document 10

# An "Act for the Better Ordering"

Even as South Carolina officials punished the rebels, they thought about how best to prevent a repeat of the Stono revolt. They settled on a legislative, legal solution. The General Assembly began deliberations in November 1739, guided by a seven-member committee. The committee recommended a strengthening of the 1737 Patrol Act (a new patrol act was passed in May 1740) and a thorough overhaul of the South Carolina slave code. The General Assembly passed an "Act for the better ordering and governing of Negroes and other Slaves" in May of the same year. This 1740 "Negro Act" redefined slaves as personal chattels (they had been considered freehold property until then), regulated behavior of whites as well as blacks, and became the legal basis of South Carolina's slave code into the nineteenth century. The act tried to curtail the excesses of slavery by placing restrictions on, for example, when and how much masters could work and punish slaves. The act also limited some of the small freedoms formerly enjoyed by slaves. Reprinted here are some of the most important provisions of the act. Even though many of these stipulations were ignored in later years—slaves still bought intoxicating liquors, sold goods, and even carried guns—the 1740 act nevertheless suggests the intensity of white South Carolinians' fear following the revolt. Note how precisely the various provisions were indexed to the events and contours of the revolt.

———————

III.   And for the better keeping slaves in due order and subjection, *Be it further enacted* . . . That no person whatsoever shall permit or suffer any slave under his or their care or management, and who lives or is employed in Charlestown, or any other town in this Province, to go out of the limits of the said town, or any such slave who lives in the country, to go out of the plantation to which such slave belongs, or in which plantation such slave is usually employed, without a letter superscribed and directed, or a ticket in the words following:

Source: From "Act for the better ordering and governing of Negroes and other Slaves in this Province," May, 1740, in *The Statutes at Large of South Carolina*, ed. Thomas Cooper and David J. McCord (Columbia, S.C.: Johnston, 1840), vol. 7, pp. 397–417.

Permit this slave to be absent from Charlestown, (or any other town, or if he lives in the country, from Mr. —— plantation, —— parish,) for —— days or hours; dated the —— day of ——. . . . and every slave who shall be found out of Charlestown, or any other town, (if such slave lives or is usually employed there,) or out of the plantation to which such slave belongs, or in which [such] slave is usually employed, if such slave lives in the country, without such letter or ticket as aforesaid, or without a white person in his company, shall be punished with whipping on the bare back, not exceeding twenty lashes.

IV.    . . . if any person shall presume to give a ticket or license to any slave who is the property or under the care or charge of another, without the consent or against the will of the owner or other person having charge of such slave, shall forfeit to the owner the sum of twenty pounds, current money.

V.    . . . if any slave who shall be out of the house or plantation where such slave shall live, or shall be usually employed, or without some white person in company with such slave, shall refuse to submit to or undergo the examination of any white person, it shall be lawful for any such white person to pursue, apprehend, and moderately correct such slave; and if any such slave shall assault and strike such white person, such slave may be lawfully killed.

VI.    . . . if any negro or other slave, who shall be employed in the lawfull business or service of his master, owner, overseer, or other person having charge of such slave, shall be beaten, bruised, maimed or disabled by any person or persons not having sufficient cause or lawful authority for so doing, (of which cause the justices of the peace, respectively, may judge,) every person and persons so offending, shall, for every such offence, forfeit and put the sum of forty shillings, current money, over and besides the damages hereinafter mentioned, to the use of the poor of that parish in which such offence shall be committed: . . .

VII.    . . . it shall and may be lawful for every justice assigned to keep the peace in this Province, within his respective county and jurisdiction, . . . any assembly or meeting of slaves which may disturb the peace or endanger the safety of his Majesty's subjects, and to search all suspected places for arms, ammunition or stolen goods, and to apprehend and secure all such slaves as they shall suspect to be guilty of any crimes or offences whatsoever, and to bring them to speedy trial, . . .

XIII.    . . . not only the evidence of all free Indians, without oath, but the evidence of any slave, without oath, shall be allowed and admitted in all offence whatsoever; the weight of which evidence being seriously considered, and compared with all other circumstances attending the case, shall be left to the conscience of the justices and freeholders.

XIV.    And *whereas*, slaves may be harbored and encouraged to, commit offences, and concealed and received by free negroes, and such free negroes may escape the punishment due to their crimes, for want of sufficient and legal evidence against them; Be it therefore further enacted by the authority aforesaid, That the evidence of any free Indian or slave, without oath, shall in like manner be allowed and admitted in all cases against any free negroes, Indians (free Indians in amity with this government, only excepted,) mulattos or mustizoe; and all crimes and offences committed by free negroes, Indians, (except as before excepted,) mulattoes or mustizoes, shall be proceeded in, heard, tried, adjudged and determined by the justices and freeholders appointed by this Act for the trial of slaves, in like manner, order and form, as is hereby directed and appointed for the proceedings and trial of crimes and offences committed by slaves; any law, statute, usage or custom to the contrary notwithstanding. . . .

XVII. . . . any slave who shall be guilty of homicide of any sort, upon any white person, except by misadventure, or in defence of his master, or other person under whose care and government such slave shall be, shall, upon conviction thereof as aforesaid, suffer death; and every slave who shall raise or attempt to raise an insurrection in this Province, shall endeavor to delude or entice any slave to run away and leave this Province, every such slave and slaves and his and their accomplices, aiders and abettors, shall, upon conviction as aforesaid, suffer death; . . .

XVIII. And to the end that owners of slaves may not be tempted to conceal the crimes of their slaves to the prejudice of the public, *Be it further enacted* by the authority aforesaid, That in case any slave shall be put to death in pursuance of the sentence of the justices and freeholders aforesaid, (except slaves guilty of murder, and slaves taken in actual rebellion,) the said justices, or one of them, with the advice and consent of any two of the freeholders, shall, before they award and order their sentence to be executed, appraise and value the said negroes so to be put to death, at any sum not exceeding two hundred pounds current money, and shall certify such appraisement to the public treasurer of this Province, who is hereby authorized and required to pay the same; one moiety thereof, at least, to the owner of such slave or to his order, and the other moiety, or such part thereof as such justices and freeholders shall direct, to the person injured by such offence for which such slave shall suffer death. . . .

XXII. . . . if any person in this Province shall, on the Lord's day, commonly called Sunday, employ any slave in any work or labour, (works of absolute necessity and the necessary occasions of the family only excepted,) every person in such case offending, shall forfeit the sum of five pounds, current money, for every slave they shall so work or labour.

XXIII. . . . it shall not be lawful for any slave, unless in the presence of some white person, to carry or make use of fire arms, or any offensive weapons whatsoever, unless such negro or slave shall have a ticket or license, in writing, from his master, mistress or overseer, to hunt and kill game, cattle, or mischievous birds, or beasts of prey, and that such license be renewed once every month, or unless there be some white person of the age of sixteen years or upwards, in the company of such slave, when he is hunting or shooting, or that such slave be actually carrying his master's arms to or from his master's plantation, by a special ticket for that purpose, or unless such slave be found in the day time actually keeping off rice birds, or other birds, within the plantation to which such slave belongs, lodging the same gun at night within the dwelling house of his master, mistress or white overseer; and *provided also*, that no negro or other slave shall have liberty to carry any gun, cutlass, pistol or other weapon, abroad from home, at any time between Saturday evening after sun-set, and Monday morning before sun-rise, notwithstanding a license or ticket for so doing. And in case any person shall find any slave using or carrying fire arms, or other offensive weapons, contrary to the true intention of this Act, every such person may lawfully seize and take away such fire arms or offensive weapons. . . .

XXIV.   . . . if any slave shall presume to strike any white person, such slave, upon trial and conviction before the justice or justices and freeholders, aforesaid, according to the directions of this Act, shall, for the first and second offence, suffer such punishment as the said justice and freeholders, or such of them as are empowered to try such offences, shall, in their discretion, think fit, not extending to life or limb, and for the third offence, shall suffer death. But in case any such slave shall grievously wound, maim or bruise any white person, though it be only the first offence, such slave shall suffer death. . . .

XXV.   . . . it shall and may be lawful for every person in this Province, to take, apprehend and secure any runaway or fugitive slave, and they are hereby directed and required to send such slave to the master or other person having the care or government of such slave, if the person taking up or securing such slave knows, or can, without difficulty, be informed, to whom such slave shall belong; but if not known or discovered, then such slave shall be sent, carried or delivered into the custody of the warden of the work-house in Charlestown; . . .

XXIX.   . . . if any free negro, mulatto or mustizo, or any slave, shall harbour, conceal or entertain any slave that shall run away or shall be charged or accused with any criminal matter, every free negro, mulatto and mustizo, and every slave, who shall harbour, conceal or entertain any such slave, being duly convicted thereof, . . . shall suffer such corporal punishment, not extending to life or limb, as the justice or justices who shall try such slave shall, in his or their discretion, think fit; and if a free negro, mulatto or mustizo, shall forfeit the sum of ten pounds, current money, for the first day, and twenty shillings for every day after, . . .

XXX.   . . . no slave who shall dwell, reside, inhabit or be usually employed in Charlestown, shall presume to buy, sell, deal, traffic, barter, exchange or use commerce for any goods, wares, provisions, grain, victuals, or commodities, of any sort or kind whatsoever, (except as is hereinafter particularly excepted and provided, and under such provisoes, conditions, restrictions and limitations as are herein particularly directed, limited and appointed,). . . . [E]very slave who shall be convicted of such offence, to be publicly whipped on the bare back, not exceeding twenty lashes; provided always, that it shall and may be lawful for any slave who lives or is usually employed in Charlestown, after such license and ticket as hereinafter is directed shall be obtained, to buy or sell fruit, fish and garden stuff, and to be employed as porters, carter's or fishermen, and to purchase any thing for the use of their masters, owners, or other person who shall have the charge and government of such slave, in open market, under such regulations as are or shall be appointed by law concerning the market of Charlestown, or in any open shop kept by a white person.

XXXII.   . . . if any keeper of a tavern or punch house, or retailer of strong liquors, shall give, sell, utter or deliver to any slave, any beer, ale, cider, wine, rum, brandy, or other spirituous liquors, or strong liquor whatsoever, without the license or consent of the owner, or such other person who shall have the care or government of such slave, every person so offending shall forfeit the sum of five pounds, current money, for the first offence, and for the second offence, ten pounds; and shall be bound in a recognizance in the sum of one hundred pounds, current money, with one or more sufficient sureties, before any of the justices of the court of general sessions, not to offend in the like kind, and to be of good behaviour, for one year; and for want of such sufficient sureties, to be committed to prison without bail or mainprize, for any term not exceeding three months. . . .

XXXIV.   And *whereas,* several owners of slaves have permitted them to keep canoes, and to breed and raise horses, neat cattle and hogs, and to traffic and barter in several parts of this Province, for the particular and peculiar benefit of such slaves, by which means they have not only an opportunity of receiving and concealing stolen goods, but to plot and confederate together, and form conspiracies dangerous to the peace and safety of the whole Province; *Be it therefore enacted* by the authority aforesaid, That it shall not be lawful for any slave so to buy, sell, trade, traffic, deal or barter for any goods or commodities, (except as before excepted,) nor shall any slave be permitted to keep any boat, perriauger or canoe, or to raise and breed, for the use and benefit of such slave, any horses, mares, neat cattle, sheep or hogs, under pain of forfeiting all the goods and commodities which shall be so bought, sold, traded, trafficked, dealt or bartered for, by any slave, and of all the boats, perriaugers or canoes, cattle, sheep or hogs, which any slave shall keep, raise or breed for the peculiar use, benefit and profit of such slave; and it shall and may be lawful for any person or persons whatsoever, to seize and take away from any slave, all such goods, commodities, boats, perriaugers, canoes, horses, mares, neat cattle, sheep or hogs, and to deliver the same into the hands of any one of his Majesty's justices of the peace, nearest to the place where the seizure shall be made; and such justice shall take the oath of such person who shall make any such seizure, concerning the manner of seizing and taking the same, and if the said justice shall be satisfied that such seizure hath been made according to the directions of this Act, he shall pronounce and declare the goods so seized, to be forfeited, and shall order the same to be sold at public outcry; . . .

XXXVIII.    . . . in case any person in this Province, who shall be owner, or shall have the care, government or charge of any slave or slaves, shall deny, neglect or refuse to allow such slave or slaves, under his or her charge, sufficient cloathing, covering or food, it shall and may be lawful for any person or persons, on behalf of such slave or slaves, to make complaint to the next neighboring justice, in the parish where such slave or slaves live or are usually employed; . . .

XLI.    And *whereas*, an ill custom has prevailed in this Province, of firing guns in the night time; for the prevention thereof for the future, *Be it enacted* by the authority aforesaid, That if any person shall fire or shoot off any gun or pistol in the night time, after dark and before day light, without necessity, every such person shall forfeit the sum of forty shillings, current money, for each gun so fired as aforesaid, to be recovered by warrant from any one justice of the peace for the county where the offence is committed, according to the direction of the Act for the trial of small and mean causes, and shall be paid to the church-wardens of the parish where the offence shall be committed, for the use of the poor of the said parish.

XLII.    *And be it further enacted* by the authority aforesaid, That no slave or slaves shall be permitted to rent or hire any house, room, store, or plantation, on his or her own account, or to be used or occupied by any slave or slaves; and any person or persons who shall let or hire any house, room, store or plantation, to any slave or slaves, or to any free person, to be occupied by any slave or slave[s], every such person so offending shall forfeit and pay to the informer the sum of twenty pounds, current money, to be recovered as in the Act for the trial of small and mean causes.

XLIII.    And *whereas*, it may be attended with ill consequences to permit a great number of slaves to travel together in the high roads without some white person in company with them; *Be it therefore enacted* by the authority aforesaid, That no men slaves exceeding seven in number, shall hereafter be permitted to travel together in any high road in this Province, without some white person with them; and it shall and may be lawful for any person or persons, who shall see any men slaves exceeding seven in number, without some white person with them as aforesaid, travelling or assembled together in any high road, to apprehend all and every such slaves, and shall and may whip them, not exceeding twenty lashes on the bare back.

XLIV.   And *whereas,* many owners of slaves, and others who have the care, management and overseeing of slaves, do confine them so closely to hard labor, that
they have not sufficient time for natural rest; *Be it therefore enacted* by the authority aforesaid, That if any owner of slaves, or other person who shall have the care,
management or overseeing of any slaves, shall work or put to labor any such
slave or slaves, more than fifteen hours in four and twenty hours, from the
twenty-fifth day of March to the twenty-fifth day of September, or more than
fourteen hours in four and twenty hours, from the twenty-fifth day of September to the twenty-fifth day of March, every such person shall forfeit any sum not
exceeding twenty pounds, nor under five pounds, current money, for every time
he, she or they shall offend herein, at the discretion of the justice before whom
such complaint shall be made.

XLV.   And *whereas,* the having of slaves taught to write, or suffering them to be
employed in writing, may be attended with great inconveniences; *Be it therefore
enacted,* by the authority aforesaid, That all and every person and persons whatsoever, who shall hereafter teach, or cause any slave or slaves to be taught, to
write, or shall use or employ any slave as a scribe in any manner of writing whatsoever, hereafter taught to write, every such person and persons, shall, for every
such offence, forfeit the sum of one hundred pounds current money.

XLVI.   And *whereas,* plantations settled with slaves without any white person
thereon, may be harbours for runaways and fugitive slaves; *Be it therefore enacted*
by the authority aforesaid, That no person or persons hereafter shall keep any
slaves on any plantation or settlement, without having a white person on such
plantation or settlement, under pain of forfeiting the sum of ten pounds current
money, for every month which any such person shall so keep any slaves on any
plantation or settlement, without a white person as aforesaid.

XLVII.   And *whereas,* many disobedient and evil minded negroes and other slaves,
being the property of his Majesty's subjects of this Province have lately deserted
the service of their owners, and have fled to St. Augustine and other places in
Florida, in hopes of being there received and protected; and *whereas,* many other
slaves have attempted to follow the same evil and pernicious example, which,
(unless timely prevented) may tend to the very great loss and prejudice of the
inhabitants of this Province; *Be it therefore enacted* by the authority aforesaid,
That from and after the passing of this Act, any white person or persons, free
Indian or Indians, who shall, on the south side of Savannah river, take and
secure, and shall from thence bring to the work house in Charlestown, any
negroes or other slaves, which within the space of six months have deserted, or
who shall hereafter desert, from the services of their owners or employers, every
such white person or persons, free Indian or Indians, on evidence of the said
slaves being taken as aforesaid, and the same certified by any two justices of the

peace in this Province, shall be paid by the public treasurer of this Provinc
several rates and sums following, as the case shall appear to be; *provided alwi*
that nothing in this clause contained shall extend to such slaves as shall dese
from any plantation situate within thirty miles of the said Savannah river, unless
such slaves last mentioned shall be found on the south side of Altamahaw river;
that is to say:—for each grown man slave brought alive, the sum of fifty pounds;
for every grown woman or boy slave above the age of twelve years brought alive,
the sum of twenty five pounds; for every negro child under the age of twelve
years, brought alive, the sum of five pounds: for every scalp of a grown negro
slave, with the two ears, twenty pounds; and for every negro grown slave, found
on the south side of St. John's river, and brought alive as aforesaid, the sum of
one hundred pounds; and for every scalp of a grown negro slave with the two
ears taken on the south side of St. John's river, the sum of fifty pounds. . . .

LVI.    And *whereas*, several negroes did lately rise in rebellion, and did commit
many barbarous murders at Stono and other parts adjacent thereto; and *whereas*,
in suppressing the said rebels, several of them were killed and others taken alive
and executed; and as the exigence and danger the inhabitants at that time were
in and exposed to, would not admit of the formality of a legal trial of such rebellious negroes, but for their own security, the said inhabitants were obliged to put
such negroes to immediate death; to prevent, therefore, any person or persons
being questioned for any matter or thing done in the suppression or execution
of the said rebellious negroes, as also any litigious suit, action or prosecution
that may be brought, sued or prosecuted or commenced against such person or
persons for or concerning the same; *Be it enacted*, by the authority aforesaid, That
all and every act, matter and thing, had, done, committed and executed, in and
about the suppressing and putting all and every the said negro and negroes to
death, is and are hereby declared lawful, to all intents and purposes whatsoever,
as fully and amply as if such rebellious negroes had undergone a formal trial and
condemnation. . . .

Document 11

# THE OFFICIAL REPORT

_f a larger report on the "Late Expedition against St. Augustine," what follows is
.ie nearest thing to an official description of the Stono Rebellion issued by South
Carolina. The report portrays the revolt as a battle between slaves' claims to life and
liberty (were the rebels the first revolutionary Americans?) and whites protecting
their "Country" and every thing "dear" to them. And, as is often the case with official versions of complicated events, the outcome is represented as preordained, courtesy of God's intervention. The report also offers information concerning the supposed
activities of Spanish spies prior to the revolt. In particular, the frequently mentioned
Spanish launch is clarified in this report. This document also suggests that what happened on an isolated South Carolina plantation was intimately connected with an
imperial, European war.

---

. . . . In September 1739, our Slaves made an Insurrection at Stono in the Heart of
our Settlements not twenty miles from Charles Town, in which they massacred
twenty-three Whites after the most cruel and barbarous Manner to be conceived
and having got Arms and Ammunition out of a Store they bent their Course to the
Southward burning all the Houses on the Road. But they marched so slow, in full
Confidence of their own Strength from the first Success, that they gave Time to a
Party of our Militia to come up with them. The Number was in a Manner equal on
both Sides and an Engagement ensued such as may be supposed in such a Case
wherein one fought for Liberty and Life, the other for their Country and every Thing
that was dear to them. But by the Blessing of God the Negroes were defeated, the
greatest Part being killed on the Spot or taken, and those that then escaped were
so closely pursued and hunted Day after Day that in the End all but two or three
were taken and executed. That the Negroes would not have made this Insurrection
had they not depended on St. Augustine for a Place of Reception afterwards was

Source: "Report of the Committee Appointed to Enquire into the Causes of the Disappoint-
ment of Success in the Late Expedition against St. Augustine," _Journal of the Commons House of
Assembly,_ ed. J. H. Easterby et al. (Columbia: Historical Commission of South Carolina, 1953),
July 1, 1741, pp. 83–84.

very certain; and that the Spaniards had a Hand in prompting them to this particular Action there was but little Room to doubt, for in July preceding Don Piedro,
Captain of the Horse at St. Augustine, came to Charles Town in a Launch with
twenty or thirty men (one of which was a Negro that spoke English very well) under
Pretence of delivering a Letter to General Oglethorpe although he could not possibly be ignorant that the General resided at Frederica not Half the Distance from St.
Augustine and in his Return he was seen at Times to put into every one of our Inlets
on the Coast. And in the very Month in which the above Insurrection was made the
General acquainted our Lieutenant Governour by Letter that the Magistrates of
Georgia had seized a Spaniard whom he took to be a Priest, and that they thought
from what they had discovered that he was employed by the Spaniards to procure
a general Insurrection of the Negroes.

On this Occasion every Breast was filled with Concern. Evil brought Home to us
within our very Doors awakened the Attention of the most Unthinking. Every one
that had any Relation, any tie of Nature; every one that had a Life to lose were in
the most sensible Manner shocked at such Danger daily hanging over their Heads.
With Regret we bewailed our peculiar Case, that we could not enjoy the Benefits of
Peace like the rest of Mankind and that our own Industry should be the Means of
taking from us all the Sweets of Life and of rendering us liable to the Loss of our
Lives and Fortunes. With Indignation we looked at St. Augustine (like another
Sallee) that Den of Thieves and Ruffians! Receptacle of Debtors, Servants and
Slaves! Bane of Industry and Society! And revolved in our Minds all the Injuries this
Province had received from thence ever since it[s] first Settlement, that they had
from first to last, in Times of profoundest Peace, both publickly and privately, by
themselves and Indians and Negroes, in every Shape molested us not without some
instances of uncommon Cruelty. . . .

Document 12

# VIEWING REVOLT FROM 1770

The following recollection of the Stono Rebellion and the nature of the 1740 Negro Act was a small part of a lengthy report prepared for the British government by Gov. William Bull in November 1770 on the condition of South Carolina. Governor William Bull Jr. (1710–1791) was the son of the author of document 7 and also became lieutenant governor of the colony (in 1759). Although there is no evidence to suggest that Bull was an eyewitness to the revolt (as his father was), he was actively engaged in the campaign against the Spanish immediately after Stono, marching against St. Augustine with James Oglethorpe. The document locates the cause of the rebellion in the assembly of a group of slaves to work on the public road (see also document 4). Bull suggests that this group formed the core of the revolt. Whether Bull got this detail from his father (who encountered the rebels but who mentions nothing about the road) or some other source remains unclear (for details of Bull Jr., see *Biographical Directory of the South Carolina House of Representatives*, vol. 2, *The Commons House of Assembly, 1692–1775*, ed. Walter B. Edgar and N. Louise Bailey, pp. 122–26 [Columbia: University of South Carolina Press, 1997]).

———◆◆◆———

There is a particular system of laws adapted to the condition of slaves called our Negro Act passed in 1740, calculated to punish offending and to protect abused slaves. The jurisdiction is lodged in two justices and five freeholders in capital, and one justice and three freeholders in inferior cases. The expence of these trials is defrayed by the public, and in order to discourage men from screening their criminal slaves from justice, a certain sum equal to the value of a new Negro is allowed to the master where his slave is executed. The royal humanity has often recommended to governors that a white man who murders a Negro should be punished

Source: Gov. William Bull, "A representation of the present state of religion, polity, agriculture and commerce," Charleston, South Carolina, 1770, Sainsbury Transcripts, Records in the British Public Record Office Relating to South Carolina, 1711–1782, vol. 32, pp. 365–406, in the South Carolina Department of Archives and History, Columbia, S.C. The version reproduced here relies on the copy in *The Colonial South Carolina Scene: Contemporary Views, 1697–1774*, ed. H. Roy Merrens (Columbia: University of South Carolina Press, 1977), p. 260.

with death. It is so in all the English colonies *north of Maryland,* where the number of Negroes is small. But in *Maryland, Virginia and all southern colonies and islands,* it has been thought dangerous to the public safety to put them on a footing of equality in that respect with their masters, as it might tempt slaves to make resistance, and deter masters and managers from inflicting punishment with an exemplary severity tho' ever so necessary.

By the happy temperament of justice and mercy in our Negro Acts, and the general humanity of the masters, the state of slavery is as comfortable in this province as such a state can be; not but there are monsters of cruelty sometimes appear, who are punished and abhorred. To the mildness of law and prudent conduct of masters and patrols, I attribute our not having had any insurrection since the year 1739, and that indeed took its rise from the wantonness, and not oppression of our slaves, for too great a number had been very indiscreetly assembled and encamped together for several nights, to do a large work on the public road; with a slack inspection; but such indiscretion is now provided against by law.

Document 13

# AN EARLY HISTORICAL ACCOUNT

Alexander Hewatt (1740–1824) was the pastor of the First Presbyterian Church in Charleston from 1763 to 1776. A Scot educated at the University of Edinburgh, he wrote one of the first historical accounts of the Stono Rebellion. Although it occupies just a few pages in his much larger work on the history of South Carolina and Georgia, the account is remarkable for both its detail and its relative evenhandedness. Hewatt was a Royalist and left South Carolina at the start of the American Revolution, and he wrote his history exiled in London. If Hewatt's account of the Stono revolt appears unusually detailed, it is because he was a friend of Lt. Gov. William Bull Jr., author of the previous document, who possibly shared with Hewatt details of his father's encounter with the rebels (on Bull's association with Hewatt, see Edward McCrady, *The History of South Carolina under the Royal Government 1719–1776* [New York: Macmillan, 1901], pp. 443–44). In some respects Hewatt's account links these primary source documents to the interpretive essays offered in the next section of this reader. The account properly belongs here, though, because Hewatt wrote near the time of the revolt and because he, quite understandably, wrote as a gentleman scholar, not as a professional modern historian. Hewatt's conventions regarding the documentation, evaluation, and interpretation of evidence were rooted in a tradition that, as historian Walter B. Edgar has noted, "showed the influence of the eighteenth-century Scottish school of historical writing in which history was supposed to provide moral instruction." But, as Edgar also suggests, Hewatt's account is remarkably dispassionate for its time and valuable in its detail (see Walter B. Edgar,

Source: Alexander Hewatt, *An Historical Account of the Rise and Progress of the Colonies of South Carolina and Georgia*, 2 vols. (London: Donaldson, 1779); rpt. in B. R. Carroll, ed., *Historical Collections of South Carolina: Embracing Many Rare and Valuable Pamphlets, and Other Documents, Relating to the History of That State, from Its First Discovery to Its Independence, in the Year 1776* (New York: Harper, 1836), vol. 1, pp. 331–33.

"Alexander Hewatt," in *American Writers before 1800: A Biographical and Critical Dictionary*, *G–P*, ed. James P. Levernier and Douglas R. Wilmes, pp. 740–42 [Westport, Conn., 1983], quotation on p. 741).

———

At this time there were above forty thousand negroes in the province, a fierce, hardy, and strong race, whose constitutions were adapted to the warm climate, whose nerves were braced with constant labour, and who could scarcely be supposed to be contented with that oppressive yoke under which they groaned. Long had liberty and protection been promised and proclaimed to them by the Spaniards at Augustine, nor were all the negroes in the province strangers to the proclamation. At different times Spanish emissaries had been found secretly tampering with them, and persuading them to fly from slavery to Florida, and several had made their escape to that settlement. Of these negro refugees the governor of Florida had formed a regiment, appointing officers from among themselves, allowing them the same pay, and clothing them in the same uniform with the regular Spanish soldiers. The most sensible part of the slaves in Carolina were not ignorant of this Spanish regiment, for whenever they ran away from their masters, they constantly directed their course to this quarter. To no place could negro sergeants be sent for enlisting men where they could have a better prospect of success. Two Spaniards were caught in Georgia, and committed to jail, for enticing slaves to leave Carolina and join this regiment. Five negroes, who were cattle hunters at Indian Land, some of whom belonged to Captain M'Pherson, after wounding his son and killing another man, made their escape. Several more attempting to get away were taken, tried, and hanged at Charlestown.

While Carolina was kept in a state of constant fear and agitation from this quarter, an insurrection openly broke out in the heart of the settlement which alarmed the whole province. A number of negroes having assembled together at Stono, first surprised and killed two young men in a warehouse, and then plundered it of guns and ammunition. Being thus provided with arms, they elected one of their number captain, and agreed to follow him, marching towards the south-west with colours flying and drums beating, like a disciplined company. They forcibly entered the house of Mr. Godfrey, and having murdered him, his wife, and children, they took all the arms he had in it, set fire to the house, and then proceeded towards Jacksonsburg. In their way they plundered and burnt every house, among which were those of Sacheveral, Nash, and Spry, killing every white person they found in them, and compelling the negroes to join them. Governor Bull returning to Charlestown from the southward, met them, and, observing them armed, quickly rode out of their way. He spread the alarm, which soon reached the Presbyterian church at Wiltown,

l Stobo was preaching to a numerous congregation of planters in
a law of the province all planters were obliged to carry their arms
ı at this critical juncture proved a very useful and necessary regula-
ʊıon. ıne women were left in church trembling with fear, while the militia, under
the command of Captain Bee, marched in quest of the negroes, who by this time
had become formidable from the number that joined them. They had marched
above twelve miles, and spread desolation through all the plantations in their way.
Having found rum in some houses and drunk freely of it, they halted in an open
field, and began to sing and dance, by way of triumph. During these rejoicings the
militia discovered them, and stationed themselves in different places around them,
to prevent them from making their escape. The intoxication of several of the slaves
favoured the assailants. One party advanced into the open field and attacked them,
and, having killed some negroes, the remainder took to the woods, and were dispersed. Many ran back to their plantations, in hopes of escaping suspicion from the
absence of their masters; but the greater part were taken and tried. Such as had been
compelled to join them contrary to their inclination were pardoned, but all the
chosen leaders and first insurgents suffered death.

All Carolina was struck with terror and consternation by this insurrection, in
which above twenty persons were murdered before it was quelled, and had not the
people in that quarter been fortunately collected together at church, it is probable
many more would have suffered. Or had it become general, the whole colony must
have fallen a sacrifice to their great power and indiscriminate fury. It was commonly
believed, and not without reason, that the Spaniards were deeply concerned in pro-
moting the mischief, and by their secret influence and intrigues with slaves had
instigated them to this massacre. Having already four companies of negroes in their
service, by penetrating into Carolina, and putting the province into confusion, they
might no doubt have raised many more. But, to prevent farther attempts, Governor
Bull sent an express to General Oglethorpe with advice of the insurrection, desiring
him to double his vigilance in Georgia, and seize all straggling Spaniards and
negroes. In consequence of which a proclamation was issued to stop all slaves
found in that province, offering a reward for every one they might catch attempting
to run off. At the same time a company of rangers were employed to patrol the frontiers, and block up all passages by which they might make their escape to Florida.

Document 14

# An Abolitionist's Account, 1847

Every body of literature has its tropes, conventions, and conceits. Antebellum anti-slavery literature was no exception. The story reprinted here was written by Edmund Quincy (1808–1877), son of Harvard University president Josiah Quincy. Edmund was very active in the abolitionist movement. He was a close associate of William Lloyd Garrison, sometimes edited Garrison's *Liberator* in his absence, and wrote numerous pieces—fiction and nonfiction—for newspapers and antislavery and abolitionist journals. The piece reprinted here, "Mount Verney: Or, an Incident of Insurrection," was signed "Dedham, Massachusetts, U.S., December 1846," and published in the abolitionist journal *Liberty Bell* (Boston) in 1847. Although Quincy's account of the Stono Rebellion—an account of the revolt unknown to most historians and reprinted here for the first time—suffers from a heavy romanticism, clumsy didacticism, and moral high-handedness, it is accurate on many details and, moreover, very much in keeping with the findings and interpretations offered by modern historians of the revolt. Yes, this story repeats in formulaic, scripted fashion the tropes of the educated slave, the tragedy of bondage, and the righteousness of slave insurrection (a favored theme of Quincy's, it seems—he wrote another essay on it in 1843, also published in the *Liberty Bell*). But we would be wrong to dismiss too readily the Verney piece as worthless abolitionist fiction. Many of the details offered by Quincy are corroborated by other accounts, and it is entirely possible that Quincy had read accounts of the revolt (most probably Hewatt's). Moreover, Quincy's story helpfully anticipates some findings on the nature and significance of slave revolts offered by modern historians. For example, Gerald M. Mullin's study of slave resistance in eighteenth-century Virginia found that the process of acculturation—how and why "African" customs changed and creolized as slaves were introduced to "European" ways in the New World—"ultimately created slaves who were able to challenge the security of the society itself" (Gerald M. Mullin, *Flight and Rebellion:*

Source: Edmund Quincy, "Mount Verney: Or, an Incident of Insurrection," *Liberty Bell* (Boston) (1847): 165–228.

*Slave Resistance in Eighteenth-Century Virginia* [New York: Oxford University Press, 1972], p. 161). This is precisely how Quincy portrays Arnold, the name he gives to the insurrection's leader. Neither is Quincy entirely romantic in his characterization of the slave insurgents. He is keenly aware of the importance of divisions among the slave rebels. The question of betrayal, loyalty, and slave rebellions is a topic that historians are only now beginning to explore fully (such was the theme of a recent panel discussion on "Theoretical and Psychological Approaches to Slave Resistance" at the Southern Historical Association's Annual Meeting, November 5, 2004, Memphis, Tennessee). Quincy writes engagingly, and the story is a good read. But readers should ask questions of this document in particular. Keep in mind that this is a story used, quite openly and unapologetically, for political purposes.

---

"Rise like lions after slumber,
In unconquerable number!
Shake to earth your chains, like dew
Which in sleep had fallen on you!
Ye are many! They are few!"
—SHELLEY

It was towards the close of an April day, (how different from those he had left behind him!) in the year 1773, that a gentleman of some political prominence in the town of Boston, found himself riding up the approach to Mount Verney, an estate lying in one of the midland counties of South Carolina. The visit of Mr. Langdon (by which name it is our sovereign pleasure that our traveller shall be known) to the Southern colonies, was partly of a personal, and partly of a political, nature. His physicians had doomed him to expiate his intemperate excesses of study and professional application, by some months of exile from New England, and the stirring character of public affairs at that time, induced him to select the more important of the Southern provinces as his place of banishment. The signs of an approaching collision with the mother country were too plain to be mistaken, and Massachusetts Bay, as the ringleader of the gathering revolt, was naturally anxious to know to what extent the other colonies were ripe for the conflict; and how far she might rely upon them for assistance in the last appeal.

It is no part of my purpose to give any particulars of his success, or ill-success, in his demi-public capacity. I will only say that, though his mission looked towards "Disunion," and even towards the possible contingency of "cutting their masters' throats," his reception and treatment were very different from that extended a year or two since, by the same sovereignty, to an accredited ambassador of Massachusetts, who visited it for the purpose of instituting a suit at law, before the tribunals of the nation, to settle a question of personal liberty. Nor will I embrace the opportunity, though a tempting one, to remark upon the folly of the Northern provinces, even at that early day, in reaching after the broken reed of Southern alliance, which has, from that time to this, only pierced the hand that leaned upon it for support. My only object in giving these particulars is to satisfy the constitutional craving of my countrymen, which would not be content without a sufficient explanation of the circumstance of my traveller being in the avenue to Mount Verney, on the day and year I have indicated.

There he was, however, and as he walked his tired horse along the picturesque road that wound its way up the side of the gentle hill upon which the house stood, he could not help contrasting the scene and the climate with what his native land was affording at that moment. Though it was early in April, the luxuriance of the vegetation put to shame the leafiest summer of his colder clime. The sides of the hill he was ascending were hung with tufted woods of the tenderest green, stretching far away upon the plain. Though the primeval forest was, in some sort, cleared from the hill-side by which the planter's mansion-house was approached, still there were left clumps of forest trees and thickets of flowering shrubs, with here and there a single tree of colossal dimensions, which threw sharply defined shadows upon the brightest and freshest of greenswards, as the sun hastened to his setting. Delicious perfumes, wafted from a thousand blossoming trees and shrubs, and myriads of birds of strange plumage and new song, and the balmy sweetness of an atmosphere which it was luxury to inhale, made the traveller feel that he was indeed transported leagues away from his bleak native coast, and bourne nearer to the sun.

Following the windings of the road, along the park-like slope of the hill, Mr. Langdon at length drew rein before the chief entrance of the mansion. It was a building of no particular pretensions to architectural beauty, excepting such as it might derive from its adaptation to the climate. Deep piazzas, their slender pillars garlanded with creeping plants, of an ever-changing variety of flower and fragrance, lent to the lofty hall and spacious apartments a shade and coolness deeply delicious. The rankness of the vegetation gave to the grounds in which it stood a somewhat untrimmed and neglected aspect, yet the place had a distinguished air and a look of tropical elegance. It seemed to be an abode where the mere pleasure of animal existence, and the delights which dwell in the senses, might be enjoyed in their highest poignancy.

The rare event of a visitor at Mount Verney was soon made known by the clamorous uproar of an infinity of dogs of every degree, and by a bustle scarcely more intelligent, of troops of curious negroes, jostling one another in their anxiety to see, under the pretence of serving, the new arrival. The master of the house, to the monotony of whose life any interruption would have been a relief, hastened out to welcome his guest with hospitable earnestness. He had heard that Mr. Langdon was in Charleston, and had written to him to beg him to take Mount Verney in his way. His prominence among the disaffected of the colony, his intelligence and his wealth, made Mr. Langdon think it worth his while to accept the invitation, although it took him somewhat out of his way. Mr. Verney ushered him into the house and heaped upon him every hospitable attention.

Mr. Verney was a bachelor of some forty years, "or by'r lady inclining" to five and forty. He lived alone with his slaves, without the solace or the care of female society. Like most men of such habits of life, he had an older look than belonged to his years, and there was besides that indefinable air about him, which gives one an instinctive consciousness that he who wears it is not a happy man; that melancholy and depression are his abiding guests. But though these fiends might not be far remote, they were certainly exorcised, for a season, by the magic of exciting and intelligent companionship. He was all animation and festivity of spirits under the stimulus of the congenial society of a man fresh from the world of life and action. He was full of questioning curiosity about that world from which he chose to live remote, and seemed to relish the rare luxury of conversation, with all the keenness which long abstinence could give.

The evening wore away in various talk, for which their common friends at Charleston, the newest gossip of the town and the latest public news, afforded topics enough and to spare. Supper time came and they were ushered by a sable seneschal into the dining-room, the size of which was curiously disproportioned to the number of the party. The appointments of the table indicated the wealth of the host in the affluence of plate and china they displayed. The viands were rather barbaric in their profusion, perhaps, than, *recherché* in their preparation; but they were none the less welcome to a hungry traveller. This repast, in those days and latitudes, was the principal meal of the day. The chase and other sylvan sports, which formed the chief business of the planters, furnished their tables with every variety of game. The yet unexhausted soil yielded, almost without labor, the choicest vegetables and fruits. The "murdered land" had not as yet began to haunt its assassins with the spectres of poverty and want. Those were the golden days of Carolina.

The repast was accompanied and succeeded by flowing cups. The cellar of Mount Verney was bid to yield up its most treasured stores, in honor of this hospitable occasion. Punch, too, the most seductive and deceitful of beverages, was there in a brimming bowl of the daintiest of china; a libation with which that generation welcomed, speeded and crowned the business of every day. Neither the health nor the habits, however, of Mr. Langdon permitting the indulgence which was the approved custom of that day, the circulation of the bottle and the bowl was made to give place to animated discourse, which was prolonged late into the night.

As the large hours began to melt into the smaller ones, they gradually concentrated their discourse on the serious temper of the times, and the portentous events which seemed impending. The probabilities of an actual contest with England, and its chances, if it could not be avoided, were fully discussed. The weight of the several colonies in the scale of battle, should battle come, was considered and calculated; which could be relied upon as firm in the faith, which were wavering, which strong and which weak, in the prospect of the coming struggle. Mr. Verney did not hesitate to indicate the radical weakness of the Southern colonies.

"Our slaves," said he, "will be a continual drag upon us. The British will forever have an army of observation, and of occupation, too, if opportunity serves, in the very heart of our country, cantoned about in all of our houses and quartered upon our estates."

"You do not think, then, that the slaves are to be depended upon in case of an invasion?"

"Depended upon! Were slaves ever, since history was, to be depended upon when they had a chance to be even with their masters? Yes, they may be depended upon for our deadliest and bloodiest enemies!"

"I cannot but think," replied Mr. Langdon, "that you do not take sufficiently into consideration the force of long habits of obedience, and the personal affection of the slaves for their masters."

"Their personal affection for their masters! My dear sir, had you lived your life among slaves, as I have done, you would know what reliance to put on that head! God knows, that I have had an experience against which no theory and no philosophy can stand!" And as he spoke a deep shade of melancholy clouded his features.

After a pause Mr. Langdon proceeded:—

"What you say is an argument fatal to the defence of your slavery. It shows it to be incompatible with the existence, or at least the safety, of any Commonwealth, where it is permitted."

"To be sure it is," replied Mr. Verney. "None but a fool or a villain would attempt to defend it on its merits. But what are we to do? We have the wolf by the ears, and we can neither keep him nor let him go!"

"It is hard to say, indeed," said Mr. Langdon, "but could you not first tame your wolf, and then let him go? A wolf may be tamed,—a negro may be civilized. Educate your slaves, prepare them for freedom, and then there can be no danger in giving it to them. Does not a wise foresight point this out as the only feasible precaution against consequences terrible to think of?"

"My friend," replied his host, in a voice agitated by strong emotion, "you talk of you know not what. Relax your hold upon the wolf, as you must if you would tame him, and he will bury his fangs in your vitals for your pains. No, no! such an attempt would be full of ruin. My whole life has been but too bitter a commentary on your philosophy! God forbid that the curse of an unreasoning philanthropy be visited upon other innocent heads!"

Mr. Langdon saw that his new friend was deeply moved by some uncontrollable emotion. He knew nothing of his history, and consequently could not divine its cause. He felt a strong curiosity to know what it was, but politeness and a sense of what was due to the evident mental sufferings of his host, forbade any expression of it. He accordingly waited in silence.

After a short pause, Mr. Verney recovered his equanimity, and turning to his guest said: "But I ought to apologize for keeping a tired traveller so long from his rest. Shall I show you your chamber?"

Mr. Langdon assented, and following his host was ushered into his apartment.

The room into which Mr. Verney conducted his guest was on the same floor with the dining-room and parlors, as they were called in those days before drawing-rooms. It had the look of having been intended, and of having been formerly used, for the reception of company. The furniture, though evidently of an age anterior to that of the inhabited part of the house, was of a style and description better befitting what our ancestors used to call a "dog-room" than a bed-chamber. The height and size of the room however made it a very fit place for the invocation of slumber, in the climate of Carolina. A journey of thirty or forty miles on horseback gave it a very inviting air to the tired traveller, and he thought he had seldom seen a more tempting object than the ample and luxurious bed, to be ascended only by a pair of steps, which reared itself in one corner, as if the appointed altar of Morpheus himself.

Mr. Verney shook hands with his guest at the door, and wishing him a good night, left him to his repose. Mr. Langdon was too tired and sleepy to take much notice of anything the room contained, excepting his couch; but he could not help observing, as he was undressing, two large portraits, nearly full lengths, of the size of life, which occupied corresponding panels, on the side of the room opposite to the bed. The one nearest the bed was of a gentleman in the dress of the days of Queen Anne or of George the First, his dark intelligent face, looking out from the fullest of full-bottomed wigs; and the other, of a lady in a fancy dress, which made it more uncertain as to the age in which so charming a shepherdess had predominated over the two sheep, which seemed to make up her flock. Mr. Langdon took but a hurried glance at them as they looked down upon him from their elaborately carved frames of tarnished gold. He bestowed one wondering thought upon them, as he climbed up to his repose, marvelling that two old family portraits of the apparent consequence of these pictures, were suffered to hang neglected in a place where they must be so little seen. But sleep soon banished all thought of his neighbor's affairs, or of his own, from his mind.

It was broad day the next morning when he awoke, (for early rising was not one of the vices of Mount Verney,) and when he looked at the pictures again in the light of the sun, he felt yet more surprised than he had done the night before, to think that they should be relegated to a remote bed-chamber. He was no connoisseur, as he had few opportunities of seeing good pictures, but a correct natural taste, assisted by personal intimacy with Copley, then in the prime of his genius, and familiarity with his works, made him sensible that they were paintings of no common merit. Especially in the picture of the gentleman did he think he perceived the hand of a master. Upon taking a more minute survey of his apartment, his surprise was yet farther increased by the discovery of a picture opposite to these, of three beautiful children—two boys and a girl,—the boys, apparently, from seven to ten years old, drawing the little girl, of four or five, in a garden carriage,—or rather the elder drawing and the younger pushing it from behind,—in all the glee and romping spirits of childhood. There was a quaintness about the look of the children, dressed according to the fashion of that day, (in the costume of men in miniature,) that struck Mr. Langdon, whose passion was children, even more than the elder portraits.

After breakfast, by Mr. Verney's invitation, he rode with him the rounds of his extensive plantation. He inspected the fields of rice and of indigo, on which depended the profits of the proprietor, and surveyed the plantations of Indian corn, yams, sweet potatoes, and other esculent vegetables for the support of the negroes, and the supply of the great house. He visited "the quarter," where the slaves lived, and saw how slavery looked in the shape of womanhood, of worn-out old age, and of childhood, more hopeless and melancholy than old age itself. Although the arrangements for the slaves were as good, or better, than he had seen on the other plantations he had visited, still there was that about the home that was no home,—sordid, cheerless, melancholy,—of the negroes, that struck a deeper horror of the system through the veins of the stranger, than all the burning toils of the field. The gardens and grounds about the house were viewed the last. At each stage of their excursion, the economy of a great plantation was explained and illustrated by Mr. Verney, whose strong native sense, joined to his long experience, eminently qualified him for such a lecture.

The ride occupied the chief of the morning, and dinner was announced soon after their return home. As they were sitting over their wine, after dinner, it was next to impossible that they should talk of anything but slaves and slavery. Mr. Langdon had a natural abhorrence of the system, which was not at all diminished by what his own eyes had seen of it. His zeal for liberty was a principle, universal in its nature and in its application, and he was deeply sensible of the disgraceful inconsistency of a contest for freedom carried on by the masters of slaves, and trembled lest this element might prove fatal to the whole movement. Mr. Verney assented to all his general principles, and had nothing to say against his deductions from them.

"What you say, my friend, is all unquestionably true. But, here are we, and there are the slaves, and what are we to do?"

"I will tell you what you may not do, if you really wish to be rid of this horrid curse, and that is—*nothing!* You are in the mire, I admit, but you can only get out of it by putting your shoulder to the wheel, and the sooner you begin, the better for you."

"It is easier to say that something must be done than to say what that something should be. We find ourselves bound up with the blacks in this infernal spell, and how to break it passes my art, I must confess."

"Were it not," replied Mr. Langdon, with some hesitation, "that the suggestion last night seemed to give you pain, I should insist on what I then said, that you cannot expect your slaves ever to be in a condition to receive their liberty, unless you begin to put them in a condition to receive it. Pardon me," he continued, seeing a cloud again begin to brood over the brow of his friend, "pardon me, if there be anything painful or improper in what I have said; for you must know that I can have no design to give you pain."

"There can be nothing improper," Mr. Verney replied, "in so natural a suggestion as yours; but I will not affect to deny that it is painful, deeply painful, to me. If I have reason to know anything on earth, it surely is the fallacy of your proposition. It does indeed touch me nearly."

Observing Mr. Langdon look concerned and interested, he proceeded,—

"I see that you are curious to know what all this means, and having raised your curiosity, it is no more than right that I should gratify it, though it be a task that I would willingly decline."

Then silencing with a hasty gesture a polite attempt on the part of his guest to waive the subject, he added,—

"Nay, what I have to tell is no secret. It is part of the history of the colony; and it is a weakness in me to shrink from what I am liable to hear of, and do actually hear of, from almost every one,—(but that is not a great many)—that comes to see me. Did you observe anything in particular in your bed-chamber last night, or this morning?"

"You can hardly think me so blind," replied Mr. Langdon, hoping that here was an opportunity of saving his host from an unpleasant personal narrative, "as not to have observed and admired the admirable family pictures that hang there. I only wondered at their being there instead of here, or in the hall. By whom, pray, were they painted?"

"They are what I meant," said Mr. Verney, with a forced calmness eloquent of deep emotion, "they are all that remain to me of my house, once an honored one in two countries. My father, my mother, my brothers and my sister,—all united in one horrible destruction, and I left alone, of the happiest of households, the last of my name and race! You can hardly wonder, my friend, that I do not choose to have such mementos always before my eyes! You will wonder the less when I shall have told you of their fate."

I shall give the substance of Mr. Verney's narrative, as it remains among the papers of his guest, in my own words, for the sake of the succinctness and brevity which the inexorable limits of this volume demand. I believe that I have omitted nothing material to the story, though I have left out many conversational digressions and explanations of the way in which the narrator obtained his knowledge of incidents, which did not come under his personal observation. I only hope that in laboring to be brief I may not become obscure.

Colonel Verney, the father of our acquaintance, was the grandson of the first emigrant of the family to the New World. His grandfather was a French Huguenot of a noble family, who was one of the multitudes dragooned out of his native country after the Revocation of the Edict of Nantz. The Vicomte du Verneuil, and his ancestors, had always been among the pillars of the Protestant faith in France. Their blood had helped swell the orgies of the feast of St. Bartholomew, and had been poured out on almost every battle-field during the long wars of religious ascendancy. For the century, nearly, that the Edict of Nantz remained in force, they were always active in the intestine broils which disturbed the reign of Louis XIII. and the minority of his successor, and in the later intrigues which gave to religious bigotry the air of statesmanship, in the act which expelled half a million of the best subjects of France from her soil. The representative of this turbulent house, therefore, had no claim for exemption, had he wished it, from the common fate of his faith.

M. du Verneuil first took refuge in England. He was kindly received, as were all his unfortunate countrymen, who escaped thither; but his very superiority in point of rank made his position more irksome to him than the humbler artizans, who easily obtained employment and melted into the mass of the laboring population, found theirs to be. He had brought away with him a remnant of his property, which, though relatively large, was very inadequate to support him and his family in the style they deemed essential to their dignity. He was soon obliged to cast about for some mode of living, which would save his pride and his dwindling estate at the same time.

About this period public attention in England was strongly directed towards the proprietary colony of Carolina. The noble proprietaries were endeavoring to revive on those distant shores the decaying feudality of the Old World. They had called philosophy to their aid, and in making John Locke the Lycurgus of their infant realm, the fantastic spirit of Shaftesbury thought they had imitated the wisdom of the ancients who made their philosophers their law-givers. But the experiment redounded as little to the Credit of philosophy, as the incorporation of negro slavery with the institutions he ordained, did the honor of the philosopher. But at the first establishment of the Constitutions of Carolina, their defects were not developed, and their fanciful structure attracted more general attention, doubtless, than a more rational plan would have done. But there was one great want yet to be supplied. Palatines, landgraves and caciques, chancellors, chamberlains and admirals, there were good store; but the proprietaries sadly lacked common people over whom these dignitaries were to predominate. Accordingly, they did their best to promote emigration by every means in their power.

The tide of industrious and worthy emigrants which now flowed from France, came very opportunely for them, and they endeavored, with success, to direct it in part towards their new colony. The names of many of the principal families in Carolina,—Manigault, Petigru, Legare, Gaillard, DeSaussure,—still bear witness to that great emigration to her shores, as the names of Bethune, Revere, Deblois, Amory, Bowdoin, Faneuil and many others testify to our own share in it. M. du Verneuil, as a man of some property, was a very desirable recruit. His attention was drawn to this Eldorado of the West by the Earl of Berkeley, and all its real and imaginary advantages set forth in golden phrase. It seemed to be what he wanted, and he was easily persuaded to embark himself, and all the fortunes of his house, in the hazardous adventure. He set sail for the New World, and arrived with his wife and only child, a youth of about sixteen, at Charleston, in November 1686.

It need hardly be said that his golden expectations were disappointed. He found a scene as different from that whence he came, as can well be imagined. But with the elasticity of spirit, and power of adaptation, of his nation, he soon conformed himself to his new circumstances, and became one of the most prominent men in the rising commonwealth. Madame de Verneuil died soon after their arrival in the colony, having sunk under the strange hardships and discomforts of her new lot. But his son, the grandfather of Mr Langdon's host, took kindly to his adopted country and throve apace in it. He married early and established himself after his father's death, at Mount Verney, then on the frontiers of the province. His name, the pronunciation of which had long been an offence to English tongues, was finally corrupted and Anglicised into Verney, a change to which he readily consented. As the colony flourished, he grew rich and increased in goods, and like a patriarch as he was, he had gold and silver, men-servants and maid-servants, and much cattle.

His contentment with his lot, however, did not blind him to the disadvantages of his position for the education of children. He accordingly sent his only son, at an early age to England, to receive his education there. As his body-servant, and in some sort his companion, he sent with him a young slave, who had had charge of him from his earliest years. Arnold, for so the slave was named from his original master, was not many years older than young Verney; but he had shown a discretion and considerateness so much beyond his years, and evinced so genuine and tender an affection, for his young charge, that Mr. Verney was perfectly content still to entrust the care of his personal safety and comfort to him. Arnold, as well as his young master, looked forward with delight to the new and strange scenes in store for them, and he felt a sense of trust and responsibility, which raised him sensibly in his own estimation.

To England they went early in the last century. Young Verney, still accompanied by Arnold, proceeded from Eton to Oxford and from Oxford to the Inns of Court. Wherever he went, Arnold was still a prime favorite both with his master and young companions. His imperturbable good humor and lightness of heart were a continual letter of recommendation, while his sterling excellencies of character won for him genuine respect. He availed himself of such snatches of instruction as he could seize by the way, with such success, that it was a common saying, among Verney's companions, that Arnold knew more than his master. However this might be, he was singularly well instructed for one in his condition of life, and might have passed muster very creditably among persons of much higher pretensions than he. In his zeal for knowledge he was encouraged and assisted by his young master, who seemed to feel as if all the intelligence of his sable satellite was but the reflected radiance of his own.

At length the time of return arrived, and somewhere about 1720, Verney, accompanied by Arnold, sailed for home. It was a great change for Verney, that from the crowds and gaieties of London to the solitude and monotony of his father's plantation. But it was a yet greater change for poor Arnold, who found himself transported from a land of freedom to a land of slaves. The kindness with which he had been uniformly treated, and the circumstance that in England he was rather better treated than worse, on account of his color, had almost made him forget that he was a slave. His return to Carolina was to him almost like a reduction from absolute freedom to hopeless slavery. His eyes had been opened and he saw his own condition, and that of his race, in all its horrors. The abominations, the cruelties, the debasement which necessarily attend upon slavery, shocked him as they never could have done had he remained always surrounded by them. The thought that he, too, was one of the victims appointed by an inexorable fate to this dreadful destiny, filled him with anguish and despair, which could not be uttered.

Gloom and despondency settled down upon his soul. The change which had come over him was obvious to all, and the old planter easily divined the cause.

"You have spoiled that boy, Jack," said he to his son, "you have made him above his business. You had better let Jones put him into the field for a while. There's nothing like hard work and flogging to take the sulks out of a nigger."

His son, however, refused to take this humane advice, and still kept Arnold about his person, as his body-servant, contenting himself with forbidding him the use of books and writing materials. He prided himself much upon his sagacity in devising this notable remedy, when it appeared, at last, to be crowned with success. After a long period of depression and melancholy, the cloud seemed suddenly to pass off from Arnold's countenance, and the weight to be removed from his heart. He addressed himself to his duties with all his former assiduity, if not with all his old gaiety of spirit. Had his master been an acute physiognomist, he would have seen that the look out of his eye, the air of his head, the carriage of his body, were all different from what they were of old. But he only observed that he was cured of the sulks, and congratulated himself on his wise prescription of abstinence from books and pen and ink.

But this change had deeper springs than the philosophy of Verney dreamt of. It proceeded from the reception of a great idea, the adoption of an absorbing and abiding purpose, for which to live. While he was plunged in the depths of his despondency,—despairing for himself and his race,—a thought flashed into his darkened mind, and illuminated its gloomiest recesses.

"Why," thought he, "are my people and myself slaves? Why do we remain slaves? Is there, indeed, no remedy? Is it a necessity, that when we outnumber our tyrants, four to one, and every one of us is a match for four of them in strength, is it a necessity that we remain slaves forever?"

The thought nerved his mind anew. His gloom passed away. He saw clearly the relative strength of the masters and slaves. He remembered that the Spaniards were at hand in Florida, ever ready to sow dissention in the colony, and to breed discontents among the slaves. He felt that a blow might be struck, which would give all the broad lands of Carolina to those hands that extorted wealth from them for others. He felt that a mind only was wanting to watch and guide events, in order to conduct such a revolution to a triumphant issue. He was proudly conscious that his was a mind capable of this great task. He looked upon the advantages of education he had enjoyed, as something providential, and designed for a mighty end. He saw himself the appointed leader of his people in their Exodus out of the land of bondage. In his excitement of thought, he saw the whole process of deliverance pass as it were before his eyes, and he beheld his nation free and happy, in the homes they had wrested from their oppressors. He accepted this natural operation of the mind, as a prophetic intimation of duty and revelation of success. His destiny was fixed. He devoted himself to the rescue of his miserable race. A deep calm brooded over his soul. He was conscious to himself that he was equal to the work he had undertaken, and he was at peace. And he had yet another seal of his fitness for his mission,—he was willing to wait!

Long years he waited. But the purpose of his soul was fixed. The deliverance of his race became the absorbing, the overwhelming passion of his being. The degradation in which he saw them plunged, the vices which were forced upon them, the barbarities which they endured, made his life bitter to him, and his only relief was in the distant hope of rescue and retribution. His character was obviously changed, but under the quiet gravity with which he performed his offices about his master's person, nothing was suspected to lurk, except the desperate contentment of a hopeless slave.

As time passed away the usual changes which it works were wrought in the condition of Colonel Verney,—for such was the rank which Arnold's master held in the colonial establishment. Death, marriage, and birth had bereaved and blessed him, according to the common lot of man. He succeeded his father in the possession of Mount Verney, he won the chiefest of Carolinian beauties to share it with him, and he was girt with growing infancy, the charm of the present moment, and the hope of future years. His political position was eminent and influential. His plantation was a mine of still increasing wealth. He seemed to have nothing left to desire.

The public duties of Colonel Verney took him regularly every winter to Charleston, and frequently to various and distant parts of the colony. On all these expeditions he was attended by Arnold as his body-servant. The opportunities which were thus given to the restless observation of the slave to discern the strength or the weakness of the different portions of the province, and to select the disaffected spirits among the servile population on whose coöperation he could rely, were faithfully improved. His manner of life, too, was eminently favorable for watching the signs of the times, and for seizing the moment, which they should pronounce auspicious. He bided his time in patience, well aware of the momentous issues of the enterprize he revolved in his mind and determined not to endanger its success by any premature or ill-considered action.

Nearly twenty years had thus glided away since Arnold first accepted what he considered a call to be the deliverer of his people, and the favorable moment had not yet appeared. At last the conjunction of events seemed to portend the hour at hand. The relations between England and Spain became every day more and more disturbed. The aggressions of Spain upon English commerce and English rights were the favorite topics of one of the mightiest oppositions that an English minister ever had to encounter. Sir Robert Walpole lingered out with difficulty his wise and pacific policy, with continually dwindling majorities, against such antagonists as the elder Pitt, Pulteney, Wyndham, and Lyttelton in the Commons, and Bathurst, Carteret and Chesterfield in the Lords. But the public mind of England was at fever-heat, burning for a Spanish war. It was obvious that the only chance of the pilot at the helm of state to retain his hold upon it was to shape his course with the tide, whose current was too mighty for him to resist. A Spanish war was inevitable.

The relations of the colonies of Carolina and of Florida were among the vexed questions which were to be adjusted by the sword. The colonies, in those days, were ever the pawns of the royal chess-players of Europe, the first to be moved, and the first to suffer, as the "unequal game" of war proceeded. The Spanish Governor of

Florida, Don Manuel de Monteano, was a man that well understood the nature of the move required of him. His theatre was a narrow one, but he was an actor that gave dignity to the boards he trod, and he was resolved to grace his narrow stage with action worthy of the widest scene. Long before affairs were ripe for war, he had been busy in forecasting preparation for it. His emissaries had been dispersed, in various disguises, over Carolina. The relative strength of the whites and blacks, the false security of the former and the necessary disaffection of the latter, were well known to him. He had that greatest of gifts in the craft of government, a wise choice of instruments with which to work.

His most confidential agent was one Da Costa, a Jew of Portuguese extraction, who fixed his head-quarters in Charleston, where he lived unsuspected, as a pawn-broker and dealer in small wares. The character of his traffic was such as brought him, without suspicion, into constant communication with the slaves, and gave him opportunities of judging which were the fittest tools for his purposes. He was too keen an observer not to single out Arnold, at almost his first casual interview with him, as the man of men for whom he had been long in search. A short acquaintance made them thoroughly understand each other, and they became of one mind and of one heart in the work that lay before them. They digested their plans they assigned to each other, and to the few confederates they could trust, the parts they were to play. A general insurrection was to be sustained by a Spanish invasion. The freedom of the slaves was to be guaranteed, and the colony was to be governed by the blacks, as a dependency of Spain. It was a good plot, well conceived and well arranged, and there seemed to be no reason why it should not succeed.

A part of Arnold's business was the encouragement of an extensive system of evasion into Florida by the slaves. This was done to such an extent that one entire regiment of escaped slaves was mustered, into the service of His Catholic Majesty, armed, equipped and paid on the same footing with the rest of the Spanish army, and officered by the picked men of their own number. The colonelcy of this regiment was offered to Arnold; but he justly considered that the post of danger and of honor, in such a perilous enterprize as this, was in the heart of the insurrection, and not at the head of the invasion. So he voluntarily remained a slave, though escape was easy, and though freedom, distinction, rank and equal society were within his grasp, that he might be a more faithful and effectual servant of his injured race.

Notwithstanding, however, the intimate relations of Arnold with DaCosta, he was free from giving him his entire confidence. He had no faith in the abstract zeal of the Spaniards for human rights, and he believed that their real purpose was only to substitute Spanish for English masters. He foresaw that his end could only be achieved by another servile war, under much less favorable circumstances, following upon the one impending, unless he could guard against this danger. He meditated the subject long and deeply. And his conclusion was one that startled and dismayed himself. He could discern but one way of permanent peace and safety for the blacks. And that was the utter extermination of the whites!

He could not escape from the terrible presence of this dreadful necessity. His heart died within him when it first stood revealed to his sight. It haunted him by day and by night. It was almost enough to stagger his resolution, and make him abandon his design with horror. The images of his master—the companion of his youth and the unalterably kind friend of his manhood—of his mistress, the beautiful, the gentle and the good—of the generous Arthur—of the frolic, mischief-loving Edward, his especial pet—of the little Alice—of all of whom he was ever the chosen play fellow and bosom friend—these phantoms made him quail for a moment as they rose before his mental sight in that fearful midnight, when this ghastly Idea first startled him with its apparition. He had neither wife nor child. All his affections centered, with passionate intenseness, in his master and his children. They were all he had to love. Was this terrible blood-offering required at his hands? His own life he was ready to pour out. He foreboded that he should not survive the coming struggle; but must he sacrifice lives infinitely dearer to him than his own? He flung himself in an agony of despair upon his face, and wept long and bitterly.

But, presently, a wail was borne upon the air through the open casement, distant but fearfully distinct. It was the chosen hour for punishment. He started to his feet. It was a woman's voice, shrill and shrieking, that reached his ear from the remote "quarter." It sounded like the "exceeding bitter cry" of his race, whose wrongs he had forgotten, reproaching him for his weakness. He thought of their blood and tears crying to Heaven for vengeance; a vision of chains and whips and branding-irons, and an endless procession of enslaved generations, rushed upon his soul. Was this great deliverance to be wrought without the dearest sacrifice? Was it to be purchased without a price? He would not shrink from his part of it, dreadful as it might be. But God grant that he might not survive the victory it was to buy.

This necessity was felt by all the blacks who were admitted into his confidence. It was agreed upon that the massacre should be universal and the future exclusion of the white race from the province the condition of its submission to the Spanish power.

Everything was ready. England and Spain were at war. The Spanish auxiliaries were at hand. The day approached. It arrived. It was a Sunday, and one of the loveliest of autumnal days. Arnold repaired early to the slave-quarter and harangued the slaves upon a case of surpassing cruelty they had witnessed the night before. A tumult of excitement was gathered around him. The alarm spread. Jones, the iron-haired, iron-featured and iron-hearted overseer approached, with two assistants, to suppress the disturbance. Seeing Arnold, whom he hated because beyond his usual authority, he rode up to him with savage glee and uplifted whip. In a moment he was stretched lifeless on the ground. His assistants met with the same fate, in the twinkling of an eye.

The taste of blood and of revenge had been given, and Arnold knew that the appetite would grow with what it fed on. He mounted the overseer's horse, and sending messengers to the neighboring plantations, led the crowd of slaves towards the great house. As they rounded the offices, and came in sight of the house, Colonel Verney was seen, hastily approaching them. His commanding figure and military bearing, acting upon their habit of subordination, checked the progress of the slaves, and they stood indecisively looking at him and at each other. Arnold saw that this was the moment on which all would depend. He rode in front of the confused crowd.

"Why, Arnold," exclaimed his master, "what is all this? How came you on Jones's horse, and what means this disturbance?"

"It means, sir," answered Arnold, "it means liberty to slaves and death to tyrants!"

"Tyrants! you rascal," replied Colonel Verney, "dismount this instant, and I will soon thrash this insolence out of you!"

Arnold dismounted and approached his master with a firm step, while the gaping crowd stood awaiting the issue. As soon as he was within reach, Colonel Verney lifted his cane and aimed a blow at his slave's head. Arnold closed with him; in an instant he had wrested the cane from his master's hand, a slight motion made the scabbard fly far off upon the lawn, the blade which it had concealed glittered in the air for a moment, and in the next it was buried deep in the heart he loved most on earth.

"Ungrateful slave!" exclaimed the dying man, as he fell heavily to the ground.

"No," replied Arnold, more to himself than to his master, "A *slave* cannot be *ungrateful!*"

I state facts. I do not propose examples. As an historian, I tell the doom which slavery once brought upon its victim tyrants. As an abolitionist, I show the only method by which such horrors may be averted. But let no one who boasts of blood shed in the battles of freedom, affect a horror at such scenes as I have described. If ever blood was spilt righteously for the vindication of rights or the redress of wrongs, that which has flowed in servile insurrection is the most hallowed of all. And let no one whose classic enthusiasm kindles at the story of a Brutus or a Timoleon, whose love of country and of freedom was too mighty for the ties of sonship or brotherhood to hold them back from imagined duty, brand as foul and unnatural murder the sacrificial act of Arnold the Slave.

The blow was decisive. It turned the tide of feeling at once. The negroes rushed forward with shouts of triumph, over the dead body of their master, towards the house. Arnold checked them, and found them willing to listen to his directions. He hastily told them that they must make all speed towards Stono, a small settlement about five miles off, where there was a warehouse full of arms and ammunition. Ten were detailed for the bloody business to be despatched at Mount Verney, under command of the only confederate Arnold had on the plantation, one whom he could rely upon to see that there was no superfluous cruelty committed. All the rest, following Arnold who had remounted his horse, hurried in the direction he had indicated.

As they hastened along the high road, they were continually reinforced by parties from the neighboring plantations, so that by the time they reached Stono they were four or five hundred strong. The little settlement was soon carried and sacked, every white put to death, and a large supply of muskets and cartridges secured. Arnold now called a halt and reduced his promiscuous multitude to something like order. The guns and ammunition he distributed as far as they would go, among those of his followers on whom he could most depend. The rest were armed with axes, scythes, clubs, or whatever other weapons their hands could find. A quantity of white cloth furnished them with banners. Drums and fifes were also in the warehouse, and musicians are never wanting where Africans are to be found. Arnold knew human nature too well not to avail himself of these appliances. So they took up their march towards Jacksonburgh, with drums beating and banners flying, in some show of military order.

Long before this, the tragedy was over at Mount Verney. The party to whom it was confided did their work quickly and thoroughly. I will not harrow up the hearts of my readers nor my own, by the details which my materials afford. Humanity naturally revolts at the horrors of slavery, whether they are administered by the masters or by the slaves, according as the one or the other have the power in their hands. It is enough to say that Mr. Langdon's host, then a child of six years old, was the only white left alive in the house. And his escape was owing to the affection and presence of mind of his nurse, who, by affecting zeal in the work, and pretending to despatch this part of it herself, managed to deceive the destroyers, until they had left the bloody scene and hastened after the main body of the insurgents. The terror of the child might well extend its influences over the whole of life. The ghastly spectacles which blasted his infant sight, when he was released from his hiding place, changed the current and the complexion of his being. He was thenceforth what these cruel calamities had made him. Such a cloud passes not away with the morning of life, but sheds its baleful shadow over its noontide and its evening hours.

Meantime the insurgent force moved successfully on towards their destination. They destroyed every house on their way, and put every white person they met to death. Unfortunately for them, they found abundance of liquor in the houses they sacked. Their chief in vain urged upon them the necessity of entire sobriety for their safety and success. The temptation was too strong to be resisted, and Arnold saw with dismay an element of failure developing itself, on which he had not counted. He hurried them on, in hopes of engaging them in some active service before they became unfit for it. Presently a small party of gentlemen were seen riding rapidly towards them. They stopped suddenly on perceiving the strange sight before them, and anxiously reconnoitred the armed mass. Arnold at once recognized in the chief of the party Governor Bull, with whose person he was familiar. The Governor saw the whole truth in a moment and, wheeling about, gallopped off with his companions in the opposite direction. Arnold, who had retained his horse for such an emergency as this, pursued them at full speed, accompanied by a few other mounted slaves. They fired upon the flying horsemen, but without effect, and were soon obliged to give over the pursuit, as the governor and his company were much better mounted than they. Here was another untoward occurrence, ominous of ill success.

A large congregation was assembled at the little village of Wiltown, in the Presbyterian church, to hear the famous Mr. Archibald Stobo preach. The preacher was in the midst of his sermon, when a sudden noise of horses' hoofs drew the attention of the audience from him. They looked towards the door, and to their surprize they saw Governor Bull enter. They rose to receive him, and Mr. Stobo paused in his discourse. Acknowledging their civility with a slight wave of the hand, His Excellency exclaimed, standing at the door of the church—"Gentlemen, a large body of insurgent negroes is close at hand. They have fire-arms, and it looks like a serious matter. Make a stand against them here, while I ride on to Jacksonburgh for reinforcements."

In another moment he was off, but the scene of confusion that he left behind him passes description. The men sprung to their arms, which they were required by law to carry with them to church, and issued forth upon the green. The screaming women and children were left within its walls for protection. Captain Bee, the principal gentleman of the neighborhood, assumed the command, and led the small force out of the village towards Stono. His own house stood on an eminence about half a mile off, and the first thing he saw was, that it was in the possession of the insurgents. They had evidently got at his wine cellar, and showed unquestionable marks of intoxication. A negro on horseback was busy among them, riding from group to group, with earnest gestures of exhortation.

It was none other than Arnold, who found his forces becoming more and more untractable and insubordinate at the very time when order and discipline were needed the most. He in vain endeavored to prevail upon them to move upon the enemy. Presently the enemy moved upon them. Captain Bee led his men rapidly along the road, and guided by his knowledge of the country, posted them so as to command the insurgents on the lawn, while they were sheltered by the trees that skirted it. Arnold saw their danger, and ordered the small body of sober men that obeyed his directions, to fire upon the enemy in their covert. As soon as their fire was thus drawn, Bee and his men issued from their cover, and passing by Arnold and his few without notice, poured a volley with deadly effect into the drunken and dancing crowd on the lawn. The panic was instantaneous and complete. They dispersed in every direction, throwing away their arms as they fled.

Arnold now drew off his command to a thicket that bounded the lawn on one side, and bade them sell their lives as dearly as they could. The numbers were now more equal, and the conflict was long and desperate. At last, on the road from

Wiltown, a reinforcement was seen approaching, which the Governor was leading to the battle-field. Seeing his chance of maintaining his ground gone, Arnold rushed out at the head of his surviving friends, to cut their way through the enemy's ranks, before the succors arrived. But it was too late. A body of horsemen galloped upon the ground. The negroes, with Arnold at their head, fought desperately, but in vain. He was cut down, and as he fell, a dozen sabres were uplifted to make his fate certain. But Governor Bull dashed into the circle, exclaiming,—

"Stop, gentlemen! This fellow must not die yet. He knows things, which we must know, first!"

He was taken from beneath the horses' feet and carried to the town, where his wounds, which were not dangerous, were dressed. This done, he was thrust into a den of torment, called a slave-prison, belonging to a private person, to spend the night. And what a night it was!

The next morning he was brought out and examined. But no word of knowledge could they extract from him. He acknowledged, and justified, his own part in this rising; but he utterly refused to implicate any others, or to give any information as to the extent of the conspiracy. He was tied up and flogged (for the first time in his life) until he fainted from loss of blood; but no syllable of information, or cry of pain, could be extorted from him. This ordeal was repeated for three days, with fresh inventions of torture. But all in vain. His firmness was unshaken. Then they spoke of pardon and favor as the reward of frankness. But the only reply they could obtain was a bitter laugh, which mocked the delusive offer of the cruelest torture of all. At last wearied with their vain attempts, and fearing lest he might die of exhaustion, they dragged him to a tree in the public square and hanged him like a dog.

He died, but his memory, spectre-like, long haunted the province. His talents and his endurance, which his examination and torture had displayed, alarmed the planters even more than the bloody effects of the insurrection. At the very next session of the Colonial Legislature, (1740,) the instruction of slaves was made a highly penal offence. The alarm was universal. Every man feared lest he might have an Arnold on his estate.

And there was reason for their fears. Not withstanding the cruel examples which were made of the captive insurgents, the spirit of Arnold seemed to walk in the province. Partial insurrections, the fruit of his labors were frequent for several years after his death, and it was not till after the peace with Spain, that the colony regained its former tranquillity.

"Was I not right," said Mr. Verney, with a mournful smile, when he had finished the narrative of which this is an imperfect sketch. "Was I not right in saying that I had had an experience that refuted your theory of educating slaves for freedom?"

Mr. Langdon could make no reply to such a question, after such a story. He wrung his friend's hand in silence. He had nothing to say, for Philosophy had not as yet taught men by examples, that the safe, sufficient, and only possible preparation for freedom is EMANCIPATION.

The next morning he took leave of Mr. Verney and pursued his journey homeward, a sadder, if not a wiser, man. He hated slavery more than ever, for this dreadful picture of its works. But while his heart bled for the blight which it had shed upon the life of Verney, he could not disguise from himself, standing as he did on the brink of a civil war for liberty, that his deepest sympathies were with Arnold.

When the Revolution broke out, Mr. Verney joined the army and rose to the rank of lieutenant-colonel in the line. He fought in many of its battles with the desperation of a man for whom life has no charm and death no terrors. But he survived all the great battles in which he had a part, to fall at length in a partizan expedition, on which he had volunteered, when on a leave of absence, in his native state.

As he died without children or kindred, his estate escheated to the sovereign people. It has passed through many hands, and has been racked and "murdered," like many an other. I am told by one who lately visited its neighborhood, that it is now a barren sand-hill, its house in ruins, its trees cut down, its fields a desolation. The pictures, which elicited this story, alone remain to recal[l] it. But it is only for their merit as pictures, that they are valued,—the portrait of Colonel Verney being perhaps the only original Kneller (except one of Jeremiah Dummer, in Boston,) in the country. They are preserved in a public collection in Charleston and admired by multitudes, as works of art. But their history is fading from memory, and it is only to a few old men, whose daily life is in the past, that they recal[l] the pride, the sorrows and the ruin of MOUNT VERNEY.

Document 15

# "As it come down to me"

## Black Memories of Stono in the 1930s

The following is George Cato's account of the Stono Rebellion as told to an interviewer—Stiles M. Scruggs—as part of the Federal Writers' Project in the 1930s. Scruggs entitled the interview, "The Stono Insurrection Described by a Descendant of the Leader." Although such narratives must be treated with care as historical sources—they are, after all, interviews conducted in the 1930s about slave life before 1865 and are far removed in time and place from slavery—a good deal of what George Cato says—roughly two hundred years after the event—is corroborated by other sources. Oral tradition among nonliterate or barely literate peoples is often reliable. George Cato stresses matters in his account that historians have come to see as critical to a full understanding of the revolt: masculinity, drink, religion, military fighting, timing. The document is the only source we have from a nonwhite perspective, and it is worth reading carefully.

————◆•◆•◆————

George Cato, a Negro laborer, residing at the rear of 1010 Lady Street, Columbia, S.C., says he is a great-great-grandson of the late Cato slave who commanded the Stono Insurrection in 1739, in which 21 white people and 44 Negroes were slain. George, now 50 years old, states that this Negro uprising has been a tradition in his family for 198 years.

When asked for the particulars, he smiled, invited the caller to be seated, and related the following story:

Yes sah! I sho' does come from dat old stock who had de misfortune to be slaves but who decide to be men, at one and de same time, and I's right proud of it. De first Cato slave we knows 'bout, was plum willin' to lay down his life for de right, as he see it. Dat is pow'ful fine for de Catoes who has come after him. My graddaddy and

Source: George P. Rawick, ed., *The American Slave: A Composite Autobiography: Supplement, Series 1*, vol. 11, *North Carolina and South Carolina Narratives* (Westport, Conn.: Greenwood, 1977), pp. 98–100.

my daddy tell me plenty 'bout it, while we was livin' in Orangeburg County, not far from where de fightin' took place in de long ago.

My graddaddy was a son of de son of de Stono slave commander. He say his daddy often take him over de route of de rebel slave march, dat time when dere was sho' big trouble all 'bout dat neighborhood. As it come down to me, I thinks de first Cato take a darin' chance on losin' his life, not so much for his own benefit as it was to help others. He was not lak some slaves, much 'bused by deir masters. My kinfolks not 'bused. Dat why, I reckons, de captain of de slaves was picked by them. Cato was teached how to read and write by his rich master.

How it all start? Dat what I ask but nobody ever tell me how 100 slaves between de Combahee and Edisto rivers come to meet in de woods not far from de Stono River on September 9, 1739. And how they elect a leader, my kinsman, Cato, and late dat day march to Stono town, break in a warehouse, kill two white men in charge, and take all de guns and ammunition they wants. But they do it, wid dis start, they turn south and march on.

They work fast, coverin' 15 miles, passin' many fine plantations, and in every single case, stop, and break in de house and kill men, women, and children. Then they take what they want, 'cludin' arms, clothes, liquor and food. Near de Combahee swamp, Lieutenant Governor Bull, drivin' from Beaufort to Charleston, see them and he smell a rat. Befo' he was seen by de army he detour into de big woods and stay 'til de slave rebels pass.

Governor Bull and some planters, between de Combahee and Edisto, ride fast and spread de alarm and it wasn't long 'til de militiamen was on de trail in pursuit of de slave army. When found, many of de slaves was singin' and dancin' and Cap. Cato and some of de other leaders was cussin' at them sumpin awful. From dat day to dis, no Cato has tasted whiskey, 'less he go 'gainst his daddy's warnin'. Dis war last less than two days but it sho' was pow'fu hot while it last.

I reckons it was hot, 'cause in less than two days, 21 white men, women, and chillun, and 44 Negroes, was slain. My granddaddy say dat in de woods and at Stono, where de war start, dere was more than 100 Negroes in line. When de militia come in sight of them at Combahee swamp, de drinkin' dancin' Negroes scatter in de brush and only 44 stand deir ground.

Commander Cato speak for de crowd. He say: "We don't lak slavery. We start to jine de Spanish in Florida. We surrender but we not whipped yet and we 'is not converted.'" De other 43 say "Amen." They was taken, unarmed, and hanged by de militia. Long befo' dis uprisin', de Cato slave wrote passes for slaves and do all he can to send them to freedom. He die but he die for doin' de right, as he see it.

# II. Interpreting Stono

Essay 1

# ANATOMY OF A REVOLT

## Peter H. Wood

Peter H. Wood, professor of history at Duke University, offered the first modern historical account of the Stono Rebellion. Wood's work—first published in 1974—has stood the test of time very well. It is the classic interpretation and account of the rebellion, and it remains the touchstone for anyone writing on the topic. Wood places the revolt in context, thinks carefully and imaginatively about causes and timing, and explains the impact of the revolt and its local and larger significance. Although other historians of the Stono Rebellion sometimes disagree with Wood, they are clearly indebted to his work on the topic. More than any modern historian, Peter Wood identified the importance of the revolt and opened up the question for further research.

———◆◆◆◆———

In September 1739 South Carolina was shaken by an incident that became known as the Stono Uprising. A group of slaves struck a violent but abortive blow for liberation that resulted in the deaths of more than sixty people. Fewer than twenty-five white lives were taken and property damage was localized, but the episode represented a new dimension in overt resistance. Free colonists, whose anxieties about controlling slaves had been growing for some time, saw their fears of open violence realized, and this in turn generated new fears.

According to a report written several years later, the event at Stono "awakened the Attention of the most Unthinking" among the white minority; "Every one that had any Relation, any Tie of Nature; every one that had a Life to lose were in the most sensible Manner shocked at such Danger daily hanging over their Heads." The episode, if hardly major in its own right, seemed to symbolize the critical impasse in which Carolina's English colonists now found themselves. "With Regret we bewailed our peculiar Case," the same report continued, "that we could not enjoy the Benefits of Peace like the rest of Mankind and that our own Industry should be the Means of taking from us all the Sweets of Life and of rendering us Liable to the Loss of our Lives and Fortunes."[1]

The Stono Uprising can also be seen as a turning point in the history of South Carolina's black population. [. . . T]his episode was preceded by a series of projected insurrections, any one of which could have assumed significant proportions. Taken together, all these incidents represent a brief but serious groundswell of resistance to slavery that had diverse and lasting repercussions. The slave system in the British mainland colonies withstood this tremor and never again faced a period of such serious unrest. For Negroes in South Carolina the era represented the first time in which steady resistance to the system showed a prospect of becoming something more than random hostility. But the odds against successful assertion were overwhelming; it was slightly too late, or far too soon, for realistic thoughts of freedom among black Americans.

The year 1739 did not begin auspiciously for the settlement. The smallpox epidemic that had plagued the town in the previous autumn was still lingering on when the council and commons convened in Charlestown in January. Therefore, Lt. Gov. William Bull, in his opening remarks to the initial session, recommended that the legislature consider "only what is absolutely necessary to be dispatched for the Service of the Province."[2] The primary issue confronting them, Bull suggested, was the desertion of their slaves, who represented such a huge proportion of the investments of white colonists. The Assembly agreed that the matter was urgent,[3] and a committee was immediately established to consider what measures should be taken in response to "the Encouragement lately given by the Spaniards for the Desertion of Negroes from this Government to the Garrison of St. Augustine."[4]

Even as the legislators deliberated, the indications of unrest multiplied. In Georgia, William Stephens, the secretary for the trustees of that colony, recorded on February 8, 1739, "what we heard told us by several newly come from Carolina, was not to be disregarded, viz. that a Conspiracy was formed by the Negroes in Carolina, to rise and forcibly make their Way out of the Province" in an effort to reach the protection of the Spanish. It had been learned, Stephens wrote in his journal, that this plot was first discovered in Winyaw in the northern part of the province, "from whence, as they were to bend their Course South, it argued, that the other Parts of the Province must be privy to it, and that the Rising was to be universal; whereupon the whole Province were all upon their Guard."[5] If there were rumblings in the northernmost counties, Granville County on the southern edge of the province probably faced a greater prospect of disorder. Stephens's journal for February 20 reports word of a conspiracy among the slaves on the Montaigut and de Beaufain plantations bordering on the Savannah River just below the town of Purrysburg.[6] Two days later the Upper House in Charlestown passed on to the Assembly a petition and several affidavits from "Inhabitants of Granville County relating to the Desertion of their Slaves to the Castle of St. Augustine."[7]

That same week the commons expressed its distress over information that several runaways heading for St. Augustine had been taken up but then suffered to go at large without questioning. An inquiry was ordered, but it was not until early April that the Assembly heard concrete recommendations upon the problem of desertions. The first suggestion was for a petition to the English king requesting relief and assistance in this matter. Secondly, since many felt that the dozens of slaves escaping in November had eluded authorities because of a lack of scout boats, it was voted to employ two boats of eight men each in patrolling the southern coastal passages for the next nine months. Finally, to cut off Negroes escaping by land, large bounties were recommended for slaves taken up in the all-white colony of Georgia. Men, women, and children under twelve were to bring £40, £25, and £10, respectively, if brought back from beyond the Savannah River, and each adult scalp "with the two Ears" would command £20.[8]

In the midst of these deliberations, four slaves, apparently good riders who knew the terrain through hunting stray cattle, stole some horses and headed for Florida, accompanied by an Irish Catholic servant. Since they killed one white and wounded another in making their escape, a large posse was organized, which pursued them unsuccessfully. Indian allies succeeded in killing one of the runaways, but the rest reached St. Augustine, where they were warmly received.[9] Spurred by such an incident, the Assembly completed work April 11 on legislation undertaken the previous month to prevent slave insurrections. The next day a public display was made of the punishment of two captured runaways, convicted of attempting to leave the province in the company of several other Negroes. One man was whipped, and the other, after a contrite speech before the assembled slaves, "was executed at the usual Place, and afterwards hung in Chains at Hangman's Point opposite to this Town, in sight of all Negroes passing and repassing by Water."[10]

The reactions of colonial officials mirrored the desperate feelings spreading among the white population. On May 18 the Reverend Lewis Jones observed in a letter that the desertion of more than a score of slaves from his parish of St. Helena the previous fall in response to the Spanish proclamation seemed to "Considerably Encrease the Prejudice of Planters agst the Negroes, and Occasion a Strict hand, to be kept over them by their Several Owners, those that Deserted having been Much Indulg'd."[11] But concern continued among English colonists as to whether even the harshest reprisals could protect their investments and preserve their safety. [. . .]

Developments during the summer months did little to lessen tensions. In July the *Gazette* printed an account from Jamaica of the truce that the English governor there had felt compelled to negotiate with an armed and independent force of runaways.[12] During the same month a Spanish Captain of the Horse from St. Augustine named Don Piedro sailed into Charlestown in a launch with twenty or thirty men, supposedly to deliver a letter to General Oglethorpe. Since Oglethorpe was residing in Frederica far down the coast, the visit seemed suspicious, and it was later recalled, in the wake of the Stono incident, that there had been a Negro aboard who spoke excellent English and that the vessel had put into numerous inlets south of Charlestown while making its return. Whether men were sent ashore was unclear, but in September the Georgians took into custody a priest thought to be "employed by the Spaniards to procure a general Insurrection of the Negroes."[13]

Another enemy, yellow fever, reappeared in Charlestown during the late summer for the first time since 1732. The epidemic "destroyed many, who had got thro' the Small-pox" of the previous year, and as usual it was remarked to be "very fatal to Strangers & Europeans especially."[14] September proved a particularly sultry month. A series of philosophical lectures was discontinued "by Reason of the Sickness and Heat"; a school to teach embroidery, lacework, and French to young ladies was closed down; and the *Gazette* ceased publication for a month when the printer fell sick.[15] Lieutenant Governor Bull, citing "the Sickness with which it hath pleased God to visit this Province," prorogued the Assembly, which attempted to convene on September 12. The session was postponed again on October 18 and did not get under way until October 30.[16] By then cool weather had killed the mosquitoes that carried the disease and the contagion had subsided, but it had taken the lives of the chief justice, the judge of the Vice-Admiralty Court, the surveyor of customs, the clerk of the Assembly, and the clerk of the Court of Admiralty, along with scores of other residents.[17]

The confusion created by this sickness in Charlestown, where residents were dying at a rate of more than half a dozen per day, may have been a factor in the timing of the Stono Rebellion,[18] but calculations might also have been influenced by the newspaper publication, in mid-August, of the Security Act, which required all white men to carry firearms to church on Sunday or submit to a stiff fine, beginning on September 29.[19] It had long been recognized that the free hours at the end of the week afforded the slaves their best opportunity for cabals, particularly when whites were engaged in communal activities of their own. In 1724 Governor Nicholson had expressed to the Lords of Trade his hope that new legislation would "Cause people to Travel better Armed in Times of Publick meetings when Negroes might take the better opportunity against Great Numbers of Unarmed men."[20] Later the same year the Assembly had complained that the recent statute requiring white men "to ride Arm'd on every Sunday" had not been announced sufficiently to be effective, and in 1727 the Committee of Grievances had objected that "the Law wch. obliged people to go arm'd to Church &[ca:] wants strengthening."[21] Ten years later the presentments of the Grand Jury in Charlestown stressed the fact that Negroes were still permitted to cabal together during the hours of divine service, "which if not timely prevented may be of fatal Consequence to this Province."[22] Since the Stono Uprising, which caught planters at church, occurred only weeks before the published statute of 1739 went into effect, slaves may have considered that within the near future their masters would be even more heavily armed on Sundays.[23]

One other factor seems to be more than coincidental to the timing of the insurrection. Official word of hostilities between England and Spain, which both whites and blacks in the colony had been anticipating for some time, appears to have reached Charlestown the very weekend that the uprising began.[24] Such news would have been a logical trigger for rebellion. If it did furnish the sudden spark, this would help explain how the Stono scheme, unlike so many others, was put into immediate execution without hesitancy or betrayal, and why the rebels marched southward toward Spanish St. Augustine with an air of particular confidence.

During the early hours of Sunday, September 9, 1739, some twenty slaves gathered near the western branch of the Stono River in St. Paul's Parish, within twenty miles of Charlestown. Many of the conspirators were Angolans, and their acknowledged leader was a slave named Jemmy.[25] The group proceeded to Stono Bridge and broke into Hutchenson's store, where small arms and powder were on sale. The storekeepers, Robert Bathurst and Mr. Gibbs, were executed, and their heads left upon the front steps.

Equipped with guns, the band moved on to the house of Mr. Godfrey, which they plundered and burned, killing the owner and his son and daughter. They then turned southward along the main road to Georgia and St. Augustine and reached Wallace's Tavern before dawn. The innkeeper was spared, "for he was a good man and kind to his slaves,"[26] but a neighbor, Mr. Lemy, was killed with his wife and child and his house sacked. "They burnt Colonel Hext's house and killed his Overseer and his Wife. They then burnt M^r Sprye's house, then M^r Sacheverell's, and then M^r Nash's house, all lying upon the Pons Pons Road, and killed all the white People they found in them."[27] A man named Bullock eluded the rebels, but they burned his house. When they advanced upon the home of Thomas Rose with the intention of killing him, several of his slaves succeeded in hiding him, for which they were later rewarded. But by now reluctant slaves were being forced to join the company to keep the alarm from being spread. Others were joining voluntarily, and as the numbers grew, confidence rose and discipline diminished. Two drums appeared; a standard was raised; and there were shouts of "Liberty!" from the marchers. The few whites whom they encountered were pursued and killed.

By extreme coincidence, Lieutenant Governor Bull was returning northward from Granville County to Charlestown at this time for the beginning of the legislative session. At about eleven in the morning, riding in the company of four other men, Bull came directly in view of the rebel troop, which must have numbered more than fifty by then. Comprehending the situation, he wheeled about, "and with much difficulty escaped & raised the Countrey." The same account states that Bull "was pursued," and it seems clear that if the lieutenant governor had not been on horseback he might never have escaped alive. Bull's death or capture would have had incalculable psychological and tactical significance. As it was, the rebels probably never knew the identity of the fleeing horseman or sensed the crucial nature of this chance encounter; instead, they proceeded through the Ponpon district, terrorizing and recruiting. According to a contemporary account, their numbers were being "increased every minute by new Negroes coming to them, so that they were above Sixty, some say a hundred, on which they halted in a field and set to dancing, Singing and beating Drums to draw more Negroes to them."[28]

The decision to halt came late on Sunday afternoon. Having marched more than ten miles without opposition, the troop drew up in a field on the north side of the road, not far from the site of the Jacksonburough ferry. Some of the recruits were undoubtedly tired or uncertain; others were said to be intoxicated on stolen liquor. Many must have felt unduly confident over the fact that they had already struck a more successful overt blow for resistance than any previous group of slaves in the colony, and as their ranks grew, the likelihood of a successful exodus increased. It has been suggested that the additional confidence needed to make such a large group of slaves pause in an open field in broad daylight may have been derived from the colors that they displayed before them.[29] Whatever the validity of this suggestion, the main reason for not crossing the Edisto River was probably the realistic expectation that by remaining stationary after such an initial show of force, enough other slaves could join them to make their troop nearly invincible by morning.

But such was not to be the case, for by Sunday noon some of the nearest white colonists had been alerted. Whether Bull himself was the first to raise the alarm is unclear. According to one tradition Reverend Stobo's Presbyterian congregation at Wiltown on the east bank of the Edisto was summoned directly from church, and since this would have been the first community that Bull and his fellow riders could reach, the detail is probably valid.[30] By about four in the afternoon a contingent of armed and mounted planters, variously numbered from twenty to one hundred, moved in upon the rebels' location (long after known as "the battlefield"[31]).

Caught off guard, the Negroes hesitated as to whether to attack or flee. Those with weapons fired two quick but ineffective rounds; they were described later in white reports as having "behaved boldly."[32] Seeing that some slaves were loading their guns and others were escaping, a number of whites dismounted and fired a volley into the group, killing or wounding at least fourteen. Other rebels were surrounded, questioned briefly, and then shot.

White sources considered it notable that the planters "did not torture one Negroe, but only put them to an easy death," and several slaves who proved they had been forced to join the band were actually released.[33] Those who sought to return to their plantations, hoping they had not yet been missed, were seized and shot, and account claimed that the planters "Cutt off their heads and set them up at every Mile Post they came to."[34] Whether the riders used drink to fortify their courage or to celebrate their victory, a bill of more than £90 was drawn up the next day for "Liquors &c" that had been consumed by the local militia company.[35]

Although secondary accounts have suggested that the Stono Uprising was suppressed by nightfall,[36] contemporary sources reveal a decidedly different story. By Sunday evening more than twenty white settlers had already been killed. Initial messages from the area put the number twice as high and reported "the Country thereabout was full of Flames."[37] The fact that black deaths scarcely exceeded white during the first twenty-four hours was not likely to reassure the planters or intimidate the slave majority. Moreover, at least thirty Negroes (or roughly one-third of the rebel force) were known to have escaped from Sunday's skirmish in several groups, and their presence in the countryside provided an invitation to wider rebellion. Roughly as many more had scattered individually, hoping to rejoin the rebels or return to their plantations as conditions dictated.

During the ensuing days, therefore, a desperate and intensive manhunt was staged. The entire white colony was ordered under arms, and guards were posted at key ferry passages. The Ashley River militia company, its ranks thinned by yellow fever, set out from Charlestown in pursuit. Some of the militia captains turned out Indian recruits as well, who, if paid in cash, were willing to serve as slave-catchers. A white resident wrote several weeks later that within the first two days these forces "kill'd twenty odd more, and took about 40; who were immediately some shot, some hang'd, and some Gibbeted alive. A Number came in and were seized and discharged."[38] Even if these executions were as numerous, rapid, and brutal as claimed, the prospect of a sustained insurrection continued. It was not until the following Saturday, almost a week after the initial violence, that a white militia company caught up with the largest remnant of the rebel force. This band, undoubtedly short on provisions and arms, had made its way thirty miles closer to the colony's southern border. A pitched battle ensued, and at length (according to a note sent the following January) "ye Rebels [were] So entirely defeated & dispersed yt there never were Seen above 6 or 7 together Since."[39]

It was not until a full month later, however, that a correspondent in South Carolina could report that "the Rebellious Negros are quite stopt from doing any further Mischief, many of them having been put to the most cruel Death."[40] And even then, white fears were by no means allayed. The Purrysburg militia company had remained on guard at the southern edge of the colony, and in Georgia General Oglethorpe, upon receiving Lieutenant Governor Bull's report of the insurrection, had called out rangers and Indians and issued a proclamation, "cautioning all Persons in this

Province, to have a watchful Eye upon any Negroes, who might attempt to set a Foot in it."[41] He had also garrisoned soldiers at Palachicolas, the abandoned fort that guarded the only point for almost one hundred miles where horses could swim the Savannah River and where Negro fugitives had previously crossed.[42] Security in South Carolina itself was made tight enough, however, so that few if any rebels reached Georgia. But this only increased the anxiety of whites in the neighborhood of the uprising.

In November several planters around Stono deserted their homes and moved their wives and children in with other families, "at particular Places, for their better Security and Defence against those Negroes which were concerned in that Insurrection who were not yet taken."[43] And in January the minister of St. Paul's Parish protested that some of his leading parishioners, "being apprehensive of Danger from ye Rebels Still outstanding," had "carried their Families to Town for Safety, & if y Humour of moving continues a little longer, I shall have but a Small Congregation at Church."[44] The Assembly placed a special patrol on duty along the Stono River and expended more than £1,500 on rewards for Negroes and Indians who had acted in the white interest during the insurrection. Outlying fugitives were still being brought in for execution the following spring,[45] and one ringleader remained at large for three full years. He was finally taken up in a swamp by two Negro runaways hopeful of a reward, tried by authorities at Stono, and immediately hanged.[46]

It is possible to emphasize the small scale and ultimate failure of the uprising at Stono or to stress, on the other hand, its large potential and near success. Either approach means little except in the wider context of slave resistance during these years. Certain elements of the insurrection—total surprise, ruthless killing, considerable property damage, armed engagements, protracted aftermath—are singular in South Carolina's early history. Yet it remains only one swell in the tide of rebellious schemes that characterize these years. In retrospect, its initial success appears a high-water mark, and its ruthless suppression represents a significant turning of the tide. But the troubled waters of resistance did not subside any more abruptly than they had risen. For several years after the outbreak in St. Paul's Parish, the safety of the white minority, and the viability of their entire plantation system, hung in serious doubt. [. . .]

Rebels from Stono were still at large in late November 1739 when rumors of new threats began. The Assembly requested of Bull that special precautions be taken for the upcoming Christmas holidays,[47] and on December 7 Assemblyman Joseph Izard departed for a week in order to raise the local militia and pursue "several runaway Negroes belonging to Mrs. Middleton that kept about Dorchester who committed a great many Robberies in those Parts."[48] Four days later the council, in a message outlining the critical situation of the white inhabitants, explained that "we have already felt the unhappy Effects of an Insurrection of our Slaves . . . (an intestine Enemy the most dreadful of Enemies) which we have just Grounds to imagine will be repeated." The council continued, "it is well known to us, that . . . if the present Session of Assembly be determined with the same unhappy Conclusion as the last," then "many of our [white] Inhabitants are determined to remove themselves and their Effects, out of this Province; insomuch, that upon the whole the Country seemed to be at Stake."[49]

[. . .] The legislature had scarcely adjourned when another potential uprising was revealed during the first week of June 1740. According to first reports among whites, this conspiracy had "the Appearance of greater Danger than any of the former."[50] It originated somewhere between the Ashley and Cooper Rivers "in the very Heart of the Settlements."[51] Its focus was apparently on the western edge of St. John's Parish, Berkeley County, near the rice-growing district of Goose Creek. This time between 150 and 200 slaves "got together in defiance."[52] These rebels lacked weapons, and they must also have had the failure of the Stono scheme fresh in their minds. For these reasons, nearby Charlestown, rather than the southern border, became their immediate objective. "As they had no prospect of escaping through the Province of Georgia, their design was to break open a store-house and supply themselves, and those who would join them, with arms."[53]

How carefully such a strike had been planned and how close it came to execution cannot be determined. It appears that the conspirators' large numbers, which must have provided the confidence for so direct and desperate a plan as the seizure of Charlestown, also proved the source of their undoing. The hope for secrecy was destroyed, in this instance by a slave of Major Cordes named Peter, and white forces had time to prepare a suitable ambush for the rebels. Therefore, according to an account reaching Georgia, "when they appeared the next day fifty of them were seized, and these were hanged, ten in a day, to intimidate the other negroes."[54] All told, some sixty-seven slaves were brought to trial, and their betrayer, Peter, appeared personally before the legislature to receive thanks in the form of a new wardrobe and £20 in cash. [. . .][55]

Further hints of slave resistance would follow. Acts of arson were suspected, and the great Charlestown fire that November did little to ease tensions. The spring of 1741 brought lurid tales of slave resistance in northern colonies, and during the winter of 1742 the Assembly was obliged to investigate reports of "frequent Meetings of great Numbers of Slaves in the Parish of St. Helena," which were still striking "Terror" into local Europeans. [. . .][56]

The Europeans' response to this "precarious" situation was desperate and effectual. Confronting at last the actual possibility of widespread revolution, bickering factions were able to cooperate in ways that maintained the English slave colony and determined many aspects of Negro existence for generations to come. [. . .]

One thrust of the white response involved efforts to reduce provocations for rebellions. Besides waging war on the Spanish in St. Augustine, whose proximity was considered a perpetual incitement, the colonial government laid down penalties for masters who imposed such excessive work or such brutal punishments that the likelihood of revolt was enhanced. Efforts to extend Negro dependence were also undertaken: it was at that time a Negro school was started in Charlestown on the assumption that a few slaves might be trained to teach other slaves certain carefully selected doctrines of the Christian faith, such as submissiveness and obedience. (The school persisted for several decades, though its impact on the total Negro population was negligible.)[57]

These gestures of calculated benevolence were overshadowed by far more intensive efforts to control and to divide the slaves. The comprehensive Negro Act, which had been in the works for several years but about which white legislators had been unable to agree in less threatening times, was passed into law and stringently enforced. This elaborate statute, which would serve as the core of South Carolina's slave code for more than a century to come, rested firmly upon prior enactments. At the same time, however, it did more than any other single piece of legislation in the colony's history to curtail de facto personal liberties, which slaves had been able to cling to against formidable odds during the first three generations of settlement. Freedom of movement and freedom of assembly, freedom to raise food, to earn money, to learn to read English—none of these rights had ever been assured to Negroes and most had already been legislated against; but always the open conditions of life in a young and struggling colony had kept vestiges of these meager liberties alive. Now the noose was being tightened: there would be heavier surveillance of Negro activity and stiffer fines for masters who failed to keep their slaves in line.[58] Even more than before, slaves were rewarded for informing against each other in ways that were considered "loyal" by the white minority (and "disloyal" by many blacks). The ultimate reward of manumission was now taken out of the hands of individual planters and turned over to the legislature, and further steps were taken to discourage the presence of free Negroes.[59]

Finally, and most significantly, authorities took concrete steps to alter the uneven ratio between blacks and whites, which was seen to underlie the colony's problems as well as its prosperity. Since the economy by now was highly dependent upon rice exports, and since the Europeans in South Carolina were dependent upon African labor at every stage of rice production, there was talk of developing labor-saving machinery and of importing white hands to take on some of the jobs that could not be mechanized. A law was passed reiterating the requirement for at least one white man to be present for every ten blacks on any plantation, and the fines collected from violators were to be used to strengthen the patrols.[60] The most dramatic move was the imposition of a prohibitive duty upon new slaves arriving from Africa and the West Indies. While Negroes had arrived at a rate of well over one thousand per year during the 1730s, slave importations were cut to nearly one-tenth this size during the 1740s, and the duties collected were used toward encouraging immigration from Europe. Before 1750 the slave trade was resuming its previous proportions, but this interim of nearly a decade meant that newly imported slaves would never again constitute so high a proportion of the colony's total population as they had in the late 1730s.

Among all these simultaneous efforts by whites to reassert their hold over black Carolinians, no single tactic was entirely successful. There is little to suggest that treatment became notably less brutal among masters or that doctrines of submissive Christianity were accepted rapidly among slaves. Despite the Negro Act of 1740, slaves continued to exercise clandestinely and at great cost the freedoms that the white minority sought to suppress. Those who wished to travel or to congregate, those who wished to grow food, hunt game, practice a trade, or study a newspaper learned increasingly to do these things secretly, and since informants were well rewarded, it was necessary to be as covert among other blacks as among whites. The result was not stricter obedience but deeper mistrust; a shroud of secrecy was being drawn over an increasing portion of Negro life.

Nor could white dependency on Negro workers be effectively reduced. The technique of periodically flooding the rice fields to remove weeds without the use of slave labor (which came into practice sometime around mid-century) may have originated in part to serve this end. But machines that could supplant the slaves who pounded rice every autumn made little headway until after the Revolution. Moreover, the recruitment of European settlers never burgeoned, despite offers of free land on the frontier. Therefore, in spite of the reduced import of slaves in the 1740s, the black-white ratio in the colony did not alter markedly.

If no one of these efforts succeeded fully enough to alter the nature of the colony, the combined effects were nevertheless clearly felt. The Negro majority, through persistent and varied resistance to the constraints of the slave system, brought South Carolina closer to the edge of upheaval than historians have been willing to concede. But in the process the slaves inspired a concerted counterattack from their anxious and outnumbered masters. The new social equilibrium that emerged in the generation before the Revolution was based upon a heightened degree of white repression and a reduced amount of black autonomy. By the time Europeans in America were prepared to throw off the yoke of slavery under which they fell themselves laboring as the subjects of the English king, the enslaved Negroes in South Carolina were in no position to take advantage of the libertarian rhetoric. Though they still constituted the bulk of South Carolina's population, too many had been reduced too soon into too thorough a state of submission. Had the earlier pervasive efforts at black resistance in South Carolina been less abortive, the subsequent history of the new nation might well have followed an unpredictably different path.

## Notes

1. South Carolina (Colony) Assembly, *The Journal of the Commons House of Assembly, 1736–1750*, 9 vols., ed. J. H. Easterby et al. (Columbia: Historical Commission of South Carolina, 1951–1962), July 1, 1741, p. 84. [The Easterby edition and the *Journal of the Commons House of Assembly*, 21 vols., ed. Alexander S. Salley (Columbia: Historical Commission of South Carolina, 1907–1946) are collectively referred to as *South Carolina Commons House Journals* (hereinafter, *SCCHJ*).]

2. *SCCHJ*, 1736–1739, January 17, 1739, p. 590. [. . .]

3. *South Carolina Gazette*, January 25, 1739 (hereinafter, *SCG*). Charles Pinckney, the Speaker of the Assembly, was reported as saying: "We consider the Desertion of our Slaves as a Matter of very ill Consequence to the Estates and Properties of the People of this province; and if some speedy and effectual Care is not taken to prevent it before it becomes more general, it may in time prove of the utmost Disadvantage."

4. *SCCHJ*, 1736–1739, January 19, 1739, pp. 595–96.

5. "The Journal of William Stephens," in *The Colonial Records of the State of Georgia*, vol. 4, *Stephens' Journal 1737–1740*, ed. Allen D. Candler (Atlanta: Franklin, 1906), p. 275.

6. Ibid., pp. 283–84.

7. *SCCHJ*, 1736–1739, pp. 631–32.

8. Ibid., pp. 628, 680, 681; cf. p. 707.

9. James Oglethorpe, "An Account of the Negroe Insurrection in South Carolina," in *The Colonial Records of the State of Georgia*, ed. Allen D. Candler, Wm. L. Northern, and Lucian L. Knight (Atlanta: Byrd, 1913), vol. 22, prt. 2, pp. 232–33. [. . .]

10. *SCG*, April 12, 1739. [. . .]

11. Quoted in Frank J. Klingberg, *An Appraisal of the Negro in Colonial South Carolina: A Study in Americanization* (Washington, D.C.: Associated Publishers, 1941), p. 68. Klingberg mistakes this incident for the Stono Rebellion later in the year. He also appears to have mistaken the date of the letter, which was May 18. See Society for the Propagation of the Gospel Transcripts in the Library of Congress, series B, vol. 7., prt. 1, p. 233.

12. *SCG*, July 28, 1739.

13. *SCCHJ*, 1741–1742, July 1, 1741, pp. 83–84.

14. James Killpatrick, *An Essay on Inoculation* (London: Huggonson, 1743), p. 56; letter of October 16, 1739, Pringle Letterbook: The Letterbook of Robert Pringle, 1737–1745, South Carolina Historical Society, Charleston, S.C. [see also *The Letterbook of Robert Pringle*, ed. Walter B. Edgar (Columbia: University of South Carolina Press, 1972)].

15. *SCG*, October 13, 1739; December 1, 1739.

16. *SCG*, September 15, 1739; October 20, 1739.

17. Yates Snowden, *History of South Carolina*, 5 vols. (Chicago & New York: Lewis, 1920), vol. 1, p. 231.

18. A letter from South Carolina, dated September 28, was reprinted in the *Boston Weekly News-Letter*, November 8, 1739: "A terrible Sickness has rag'd here, which the Doctors call a yellow bilious Fever, of which we bury 8 or 10 in a Day; the like never known among us; but seems to abate as the cold Weather advances."

19. *SCG*, August 18, 1739.

20. May 5, 1724, Sainsbury Transcripts, Records in the British Public Record Office Relating to South Carolina, 1663–1782, London.

21. *SCCHJ*, 1724, June 4, 1724, pp. 7, 9; *SCCHJ*, 1726–1727, January 13, 1727, p. 69.

22. *SCG*, March 26, 1737. It is significant that the next set of presentments dealt with the other side of the coin. It was objected in October that the Sabbath laws were being violated "in several Parts of the Country by laying Negroes under a Necessity of Labouring on that Day, contrary to the Laws of God and Man"; *SCG*, November 5, 1737. Whether Sunday labor reduced or enhanced the prospects of rebellion would be debated repeatedly by whites in the next several years.

23. A similar law, which made clear provisions for the security of Charlestown, was passed in 1743. *The Statutes at Large of South Carolina*, 10 vols., ed. Thomas Cooper and David J. McCord (Columbia, S.C.: Johnston, 1836–1841), vol. 7, p. 417–19.

24. "The Journal of William Stephens," p. 412. A confirmation that war had been declared and the first news of an insurrection at Stono reached Georgia before noon, September 13, via the same "express" from Charlestown.

25. U. B. Phillips (*American Negro Slavery* [New York & London: Appleton, 1918], p. 473) gives the leader's name as Jonny. [Herbert] Aptheker points out in *American Negro Slave Revolts* (New York: Columbia University Press, 1943), p. 187 n., that Dr. Ramsey called the leader Cato and used the date 1740. (He could have been referring to a later incident mentioned below.) To avoid such confusions, I have bypassed derivative secondary sources and pieced together the following description of the Stono Uprising from the contemporary materials that survive.

26. "Account of the Negroe Insurrection," p. 234. This would suggest that even in the midst of the most desperate revolt, slave violence was by no means haphazard. [. . .]

27. Ibid.

28. Ibid.

29. Ibid. Miles Mark Fisher, *Negro Slave Songs in the United States* (Ithaca, N.Y.: Cornell University Press, 1953), p. 70, points out that members of secret West African cults often claimed invincible powers from the presence of a special banner (much as Roman legions or American Marines have historically drawn inspiration from the sight of certain standards):

> Negro cultists in many instances acted as though they were invulnerable. A picture of one of their banners in Africa, drawn by a slave trader of the eighteenth century, shows the cultist carrying a large grigri bag. In it were charms to preserve one from hurt or harm. . . . Jemmy's insurrectionists in South Carolina in the eighteenth century and the Vesey plotters of the same area in the nineteenth century were reckless because of their dependence upon their banners.

Cf. William C. Suttles Jr., "African Religious Survivals as Factors in American Slave Revolts," *Journal of Negro History* 56 (1971): 97–104.

30. Alexander Hewatt, *An Historical Account of the Rise and Progress of the Colonies of South Carolina and Georgia*, 2 vols. (London: Donaldson, 1779), rpt. in *Historical Collections of South Carolina*, ed. B. R. Carroll (New York: Harper, 1836), vol. 1, p. 332. The account in Edward McCrady, *The History of South Carolina under the Royal Government, 1719–1776* (New York: Macmillan, 1901), pp. 185–86, which follows Hewatt, suggests that Bull went to Charlestown via John's Island while a companion named Golightly rode the eight miles to Wiltown church.

31. Henry A. M. Smith, "Willtown or New London," *South Carolina Historical and Genealogical Magazine* 10 (1909): 28.

32. "Account of the Negroe Insurrection," p. 235. One slave was said to have answered his owner's query as to whether he truly wished to kill his master by pulling the trigger on his pistol, only to have the weapon misfire, at which the planter shot him through the head. "A Ranger's Report of Travels with General Oglethorpe, 1739–1742," in *Travels in the American Colonies*, ed. Newton D. Mereness (New York: Macmillan, 1916), p. 223.

33. "Account of the Negroe Insurrection," p. 235.

34. "A Ranger's Report," p. 223.

35. *SCCHJ*, 1739–1741, p. 158.

36. This version is repeated in M. Eugene Sirmans, *Colonial South Carolina: A Political History, 1663–1763* (Chapel Hill: University of North Carolina Press, 1966), pp. 207–8, and it has recently been echoed again in Richard Hofstadter, *America at 1750: A Social Portrait* (New York: Knopf, 1971), p. 129.

37. "The Journal of William Stephens," p. 412; cf. "A Ranger's Report," p. 222, which says "about forty White People" died.

38. *Boston Weekly News-Letter*, November 8, 1739, extract of a letter from South Carolina dated September 28.

39. Andrew Leslie to Philip Bearcroft, St. Paul's Parish, S.C., January 7, 1740, quoted in Klingberg, *Appraisal*, p. 80.

40. *Boston Weekly News-Letter*, November 30, 1739. Although the printer put August 18, the date on the letter from South Carolina must have been October 18 or thereabouts. The correspondent added: "The Yellow Fever is abated, but has been very mortal."

41. "The Journal of William Stephens," p. 427; cf. "A Ranger's Report," p. 222.

42. "Account of the Negroe Insurrection," p. 236.

43. *SCCHJ*, 1739–1741, November 21, 1739, p. 37.

44. Letter of Andrew Leslie cited in note 39 above.

45. *SCCHJ*, 1739–1741, pp. 341, 528–29.

46. *SCG*, December 27, 1742; *SCCHJ*, 1742–1744, p. 263.

47. *SCCHJ*, 1739–1741, p. 69.

48. Ibid., p. 84.

49. Ibid., p. 97. The previous session of the Assembly had ended without passage of a new Negro Act.

50. "The Journal of William Stephens," p. 592.

51. *SCCHJ*, 1739–1741, p. 364.

52. "The Journal of William Stephens," p. 592.

53. Benjamin Martyn, *An Impartial Inquiry into the State and Utility of the Province of Georgia* (London: Meadows, 1741), p. 173.

54. Ibid.

55. *SCCHJ*, 1739–1741, p. 480. [. . .]

56. *SCCHJ*, 1741–1742, February 17, 1742, p. 388; cf. pp. 381–82.

57. Sirmans, *Colonial South Carolina*, p. 210; cf. p. 142.

58. *Statutes*, ed. Cooper and McCord, vol. 7, p. 397–417.

59. *SCCHJ*, 1739–1741, pp. 325–26.

60. For example, in May 1744 Peter Taylor was fined £10 "for keeping Slaves without a white Person"; *SCCHJ*, 1744–1745, p. 147.

Essay 2

# AFRICAN DIMENSIONS

## John K. Thornton

Seventeen years after Peter Wood wrote his account of the revolt, John K. Thornton of Boston University offered the first sustained revision of Wood's work. Thornton brought the interpretative skills and knowledge of a historian of Africa and the Atlantic world to the Stono Rebellion. Thornton's compelling essay draws on English and Portuguese sources to establish the connections between events at Stono in 1739 and the history of West Africa. The essay makes a very persuasive case for understanding the revolt in terms of its "African" dimensions. As Thornton shows, the rebels at Stono were likely Kongolese in origin, a link that helps us understand why they revolted and how they fought.

---

The Stono Rebellion of 1739 was one of the largest and costliest in the history of the United States. In studying it, historians have generally not appreciated the extent to which the African background of the participants may have shaped their decision to revolt or their subsequent actions. This essay addresses the upheaval in South Carolina in terms of its African background and attempts to show that understanding the history of the early-eighteenth-century kingdom of Kongo can contribute to a fuller view of the slaves' motivations and actions.

In some ways, the failure to consider the African background of the revolt is surprising, since a number of historians have recently explored the possibility of African religions, cultures, and societies playing an important role in other aspects of South Carolina life. Peter Wood, author of the richest examination of Stono, was one of the pioneers in considering African competence at rice growing as important in shaping the decisions of slave buyers, a point followed up in great detail by Daniel Littlefield.[1] Wood also argued that the African origins of the slaves can do much to explain a range of behaviors, from health patterns to language.[2] Tom Shick showed that African concepts of health and healing influenced the development of

Source: John K. Thornton, "African Dimensions of the Stono Rebellion," *American Historical Review* 96 (October 1991): 1101–13. The edited version of the essay appears here by permission of the author and the American Historical Association.

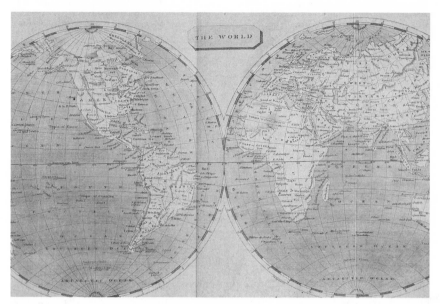

"The World." From Aaron Arrowsmith, *A New and Elegant General Atlas, Comprising All the New Discoveries, to the Present Time; Containing Sixty-three Maps, Drawn by Arrowsmith and Lewis* (Philadelphia: J. Conrad, 1804), map 1. Courtesy of the South Caroliniana Library, University of South Carolina.

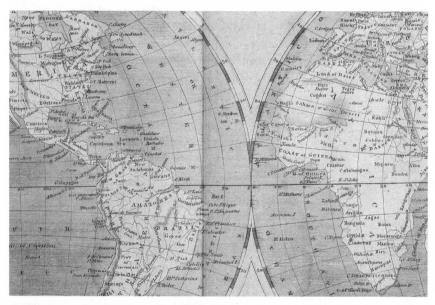

Detail of the coasts of Africa, North America, and South America. From Aaron Arrowsmith, *A New and Elegant General Atlas, Comprising All the New Discoveries, to the Present Time; Containing Sixty-three Maps, Drawn by Arrowsmith and Lewis* (Philadelphia: J. Conrad, 1804), map 1. Courtesy of the South Caroliniana Library, University of South Carolina.

folk medicine in South Carolina, and Margaret Washington Creel ex
gious development in terms of African religion and religiosity.[3]

Historians have yet to apply the same sort of approach to the Stono
Scholars of the United States interested in the African background of American history have usually sought general information about African culture by reading the
accounts of modern anthropologists and ethnologists, which are not always helpful for understanding specific historical situations. Appreciating the African roots of
the Stono Rebellion, for example, requires a specific understanding of the kingdom
of Kongo between 1680 and 1740 rather than simply a broad understanding of
African culture. Historians of Africa, who have access to this type of specific information, have, unfortunately, rarely used it in a way helpful to their colleagues in
U.S. history.[4]

Although the Stono Rebellion was very important in the history of South Carolina, it was not well documented. Only one eyewitness account is extant, supplemented by several secondhand reports.[5] Many English residents of South Carolina,
including the anonymous author of the best account, believed that the revolt was
somehow precipitated by Spanish propaganda and was part of the larger set of tensions that led to war between England and Spain in 1740. English officials reported
a number of Spanish vessels acting suspiciously in English waters, and some
Spaniards, including priests, were reported to have made surreptitious visits to
South Carolina.[6] Among other things, these Spaniards were believed to be stirring
up the slaves, offering freedom to any who would run away, as indeed many did.[7]

The actual rebellion broke out on Sunday (normally a slave's day off), September 9, 1739, led by a man named Jemmy and including a core of some twenty
"Angolan" slaves. The Spanish were suspected in the uprising because, according to
the account, the slaves were Catholics, and "the Jesuits have a mission and school
in that Kingdom [Angola] and many Thousands of the Negroes profess the Roman
Catholic Religion." In addition to the sentiments of a common religion, many
slaves could speak Portuguese, which was "as near Spanish as Scotch is to English,"[8]
thus increasing their receptivity to Spanish offers and propaganda.

The rebels seized a store of firearms and marched off on a trail of destruction
and killing, with two drums and banners flying, which attracted a large crowd of
slaves. Having reached over sixty in number, they paused at a large field and "set to
dancing, Singing and beating Drums to draw more Negroes to them." Shortly after-
ward, now numbering ninety, they met a force of militia, and a battle resulted. The
slaves were dispersed, though not without "acting boldly" and leaving some dead.[9]
The slaves were not finished, however, for they re-formed and continued toward
the Spanish possessions around St. Augustine, one body of about ten fleeing until
caught by mounted troops the next day.[10] A week later, another group fought a
pitched battle with pursuing militia about thirty miles south of the initial skirmish.[11]

While the immediate causes of the revolt clearly lay in the difficult conditions of slavery in South Carolina, detailed in Wood's analysis of the colony and the revolt,[12] several elements in the eyewitness account suggest that, along with English mistreatment and Spanish promises, the African background of the slaves contributed to the nature of the revolt. A study of the African background supports the following interpretation: first, South Carolina slaves were in all likelihood not drawn from the Portuguese colony of Angola (as the account implies) but from the kingdom of Kongo (in modern Angola), which was a Christian country and had a fairly extensive system of schools and churches in addition to a high degree of literacy (at least for the upper class) in Portuguese. In its Creole form, Portuguese was also a widely used language of trade as well as the second language of educated Kongolese. The Kongolese were proud of their Christian and Catholic heritage, which they believed made them a distinctive people, and thus Kongolese slaves would have seen the Spanish offers in terms of freedom of religion (or rather, freedom of Catholic religion) as additionally attractive beyond promises of freedom in general.

Second, throughout the eighteenth century, Kongo was disturbed by sporadic and sometimes lengthy civil wars, which resulted in the capture and sale of many people, no small number of whom would have been soldiers with military training. Significant changes in the organization and training of armies that were occurring at the same time had increased the number of soldiers trained in the use of firearms, thus increasing the likelihood that such soldiers would be enslaved. These ex-soldiers might contrast with the untrained villagers often netted by slave raids, judicial enslavement, or other means by which slaves ended up being sold to the Americas. Former soldiers might have provided the military core of the rebels, who fought on after their first engagement and generally gave a good account of themselves.

From patterns of the English slave trade to central Africa, we know it is unlikely that the "Kingdom of Angola" to which the author of the main account of the Stono Rebellion referred was the Portuguese colony known as Angola, largely because the colony sent its slaves on Portuguese and Brazilian ships to Brazil and not to English shipping bound for North America.[13] Rather, the author surely meant the general stretch of central Africa known to English shippers as the Angola coast. This area included coastal parts of modern Zaire, Congo-Brazzaville, and Gabon as well as Angola. The English slave trade, conducted in this period by the Royal African Company, fixed its operations on the northern part of the coast, especially at the town of Kabinda, just north of the mouth of the Zaire River.[14] The importance of Kabinda is underscored by the fact that, according to company records, every central African voyage the company undertook in the 1720s gave Kabinda as its destination.[15] Kabinda was the capital of an independent state, which, lying as it did against a sparsely inhabited interior, did not procure many slaves itself but served as an export station for suppliers coming from the south. Since Kabinda's first line of supply was its southern neighbor across the Zaire, the "Angolans" of the Stono Rebellion most likely came from Kongo. Eighteenth-century visitors such as James Barbot often left from Kabinda to visit other ports along the Kongo coast to the south or up the Zaire River to the town of Nzari (Zaire).[16] Accounts of the 1760s refer to a brisk trade in Kongo's province of Mbula lying on the Zaire and upstream of Nzari, which supplied English, French, and Dutch merchants (probably based at Kabinda) as well.[17]

The possibility that people from other parts of central Africa were involved in the rebellion cannot be completely ruled out, however, since Kabinda was also served by the Vili trading network. Centered in the kingdom of Loango, farther north up the coast, Vili traders had built a series of towns since at least the mid-seventeenth century under a disciplined caravan system across Kongo that supplied many of their slaves,[18] but they also contacted suppliers outside Kongo. The Vili engaged in trade with Portuguese Angola despite colonial attempts to prohibit it, and they dealt extensively with Matamba, Angola's independent eastern neighbor. [. . .][19]

Thus merchants based at Kabinda would buy slaves from an extensive area of central Africa. Nevertheless, the majority enslaved in the period between about 1710 and 1740 were probably from Kongo. First of all, the kingdom was the principal supplier to Kabinda-based merchants and to Vili merchants as well. Second, the eastern regions served by merchants in Nzombo and the Malebo Pool were not as fully engaged in the slave trade in the early eighteenth century as they would become by midcentury, especially after the arrival of Lunda armies in the Kwango region around 1750. Third, the southern regions were jealously guarded by the Portuguese authorities, who sought to block trade northward with a fort at Nkoje built in 1759 specifically to stop Vili traders.[20] Even though the Portuguese could not stop northbound trade completely—it continued to reach Kabinda by overland or coastal routes and French, English, and Dutch merchants based on the north coast—they probably did limit it considerably.

The background of trade points strongly to a Kongo origin of the Stono slaves, but it is their adherence to Catholicism that confirms it. Only two countries in central Africa were Christian: Kongo and the Portuguese colony of Angola. Missionaries based in Angola did some work in eastern areas outside colonial control, such as Matamba, but they were limited by a shortage of missionaries in the eighteenth century.[21] Even in the best of times, these missions were typically of short duration and did not lead to the establishment of a long-lasting, permanent church organization.[22] In eastern Angola, moreover, admission of missionaries and acceptance of baptism was usually linked to surrender to Portugal, which slowed missionary work and restricted mass conversions.[23] The slaves from the east of Kongo, supplied by Nzombo or Vili merchants, were definitely not Christians according to the Italian Capuchin missionary in Kongo, Cherubino da Savona, who referred to them as "heathens."[24]

Of these two Christian countries, Angola was unlikely to export slaves to English ships, especially Christian slaves who would surely have been drawn from areas under direct Portuguese control, where Portuguese restrictions were strongest. That Christian slaves in English hands would be from Kongo is substantiated by complaints of the Spanish Governor Antonio de Salas of New Granada (Colombia) to the Spanish crown in 1735. He stated that English merchants representing the South Sea Company (drawing on the same sources as the English supplying South Carolina) were introducing "black Christians of the Congo" into Cartagena.[25]

These same "black Christians of the Congo" were the leading rebels of the Stono Rebellion, susceptible to Spanish and Catholic propaganda. They came from a culture well disposed toward Catholics. The Kongolese of the eighteenth century regarded their Christianity as a fundamental part of their national identity,[26] since the kingdom was voluntarily converted with the baptism of King Nzinga Nkuwu as João I in 1491, not linked to submission to Portugal as many of the eastern Angolan conversions were. It had independent relations with Rome and its own internally developed church and school system.[27]

This locally rooted Christian tradition is sometimes regarded as less than orthodox. Most modern scholars have pointed out that the Kongolese simply added Christian labels to their indigenous beliefs. Foreign clergy who worked in Kongo in the seventeenth and eighteenth centuries often regarded them as "Christians in name only," although some other accounts praise them as model Christians.[28] But, whatever modern scholars or some eighteenth-century priests thought, the Kongolese regarded themselves as Christians. The elite carefully maintained chapels and sent their children to schools, and the ordinary people learned their prayers and hymns, even in the eighteenth century, when ordained clergy were often absent.[29] Even those priests who doubted the orthodoxy of the Kongolese did not doubt their sincerity, since, as priests, they were often surrounded by crowds of people singing hymns or demanding their children be baptized. The high wooden crosses that marked Kongolese chapels could still be seen in the twentieth century.[30] These observations by travelers in Africa were seconded by occasional clerical observations in the Americas, where Kongolese slaves were well known to be Christians.[31] The same was true in Spanish Florida, for, in 1748, a free Kongolese, Miguel Domingo, told the priest at Gracia Real de Santa Teresa de Mose that he had been baptized and continued to pray in Kikongo, probably using prayers like those printed in the Kikongo catechism of 1624.[32]

In many ways, acceptance of the Portuguese language as the official language of the kingdom of Kongo paralleled the acceptance of Christianity. The author of the account of the Stono Rebellion believed that the slaves were especially open to Spanish propaganda because some could speak its Iberian sister language, and at least some Kongolese slaves could indeed do this. Almost from the start of European contacts, the Kongolese developed literacy in Portuguese: the first letter composed by a literate Kongolese dated from 1491.[33] Schools developed rapidly in Kongo, and by the seventeenth century there was a school in every major provincial capital.[34] Literacy was more or less restricted to the upper class, but the fact that Kongo's archives and official documents were written in Portuguese helped create a general familiarity with the language among the ordinary people.[35]

More important for the people, undoubtedly, was the dominance of Portuguese in the language of trade, not just in Kongo but in the whole of west-central Africa.[36] The status of Portuguese (or rather, creole Portuguese) as a trade language did not mean that all, or even most, Kongolese could speak Portuguese; in fact, governors of Angola complained that even citizens of the colony seemed to prefer African languages to Portuguese at home.[37] But it did mean that among any sizable group of Kongolese slaves there were likely to be bilingual speakers. During an earlier period, Jesuit missionaries in America had routinely used bilingual Kongolese as catechists.[38] Thus, in the context of colonial South Carolina, Spanish agents were quite likely to be able to communicate with at least some Kongolese slaves, who could in turn communicate with others who knew no Portuguese.

The slaves fought well in the various military engagements that made up the Stono Rebellion. This may have been a result of their bravery and desperation, or they may have acquired military skills as soldiers of the colonies. In the Americas, slaves did sometimes serve in the colonial militia, and they may have been trained there. Wood examined the issue, however, and pointed out that militia service for slaves, while common in the earlier periods, had been phased out by the 1720s. By that time, South Carolina had already passed strong restrictions against slaves possessing firearms, and slaves no longer served in the militia, although many probably still had access to guns for hunting.[39]

Military service in Africa may well have served a more important role than occasional militia service or hunting. Considering that many slaves were first captured in wars, it is reasonable to assume that some of the rebels had been soldiers.[40] Of course, not every person enslaved during military action in Kongo was a soldier. Often, armed forces raided villages, carrying off civilians who would then be sold into slavery. [. . .] There were many other ways to become enslaved—kidnapping, judicial punishment, or indebtedness. Any of these methods might capture a civilian with no knowledge of military affairs at all. Soldiers were only captured in wars, wars that ranged armies against each other. However, eighteenth-century Kongo had plenty of wars.

Before 1665, Kongo was a centralized kingdom, one in which there was a great deal of internal order. If Kongolese were enslaved, it would be as a result of external attack, not internal disorder; consequently, relatively few Kongolese were enslaved before the mid-seventeenth century.[41] After 1665, all this changed, as civil wars raged almost constantly for the next forty-four years. While the causes and development of the wars need not concern us here, it is enough to note that fairly large-scale engagements between Kongolese armies were commonplace. [. . . S]everal incidents in the 1730s are clearly indicative of major wars during that period. For example, a Capuchin priest, Angelo Maria da Polinago, visiting Kongo's coastal principality of Nsoyo in 1733, noted that he was prevented from traveling to the southern areas (in the duchy of Mbamba) because of a major war in that area.[42] Soldiers captured in this war, or others like it that are not documented, would certainly be exported, via Kabinda to Spanish Cartagena or to South Carolina by the English companies.

Some features of the account of the Stono Rebellion suggest that Kongolese soldiers taken as slaves in this and other, undocumented, wars of the 1730s were among the rebels at Stono. For example, the rebels quickly seized a supply of guns and apparently handled them well.[43] The utility of guns in a revolt is directly proportional to the skill with which the rebels are capable of using them, and this, in turn, is dependent on training. Presumably, those unfamiliar with guns might have sought other weapons, such as knives, axes, or agricultural tools, and passed up a raid on an armory. Because the colonial militia did not provide much in the way of firearms training, the possibility of an African source of training seems more likely.

Kongolese soldiers would certainly have had training with modern weapons. By the early eighteenth century, guns were becoming more and more common on African battlefields, and skill in their use was being passed on to a larger and larger group of soldiers. A military revolution was altering war in Kongo and other parts of Africa, increasing the size of armies, and replacing the hand-to-hand combat of lances, swords, and axes with the missile combat of muskets. [. . .]

Not only were muskets used by a greater percentage of soldiers than before, but the use of trained military forces had also spread to outlying areas and led to recruitment of more soldiers among the population. At its height, Kongo's army was centralized: the authorities in the capital (São Salvador) had most of the soldiers, while the provincial nobility possessed relatively small guard units.[44] But after the civil wars began in Kongo, armed retinues became essential in even small provinces and towns. Tomassi da Cortona noted that the duke of Mbamba had a fairly large standing army in 1734, and his contemporary, Angelo Maria da Polinago, observed that even the small marquisate of Kitombo mustered a considerable force of soldiers to greet him in 1733.[45] Thus, although the size of any given army probably fell during the period 1665 to 1740, as a result of the decentralization of power the total number of people under arms and receiving military training with firearms probably rose.[46]

In addition to handling firearms in a way that suggests military training, the Stono rebels also gave other indications of an African military background. For example, they marched under banners like the unit flags that African armies flew in their campaigns,[47] and they used drums to encourage the rebels. Of course, such behavior might simply have been imitative of colonial militias in which Africans may still have served or at the very least observed. Far more significant was the fact that the rebels danced.[48] Their dancing need not have been simply a reflection of the joy of the prospect of freedom or the result of drunkenness. Although European and Euro-American armies and militias marched, flew flags, and beat drums as they approached combat, they did not dance. Military dancing was a part of the African culture of war. In African war, dancing was as much a part of military preparation as drill was in Europe. Before 1680, when soldiers fought hand to hand, dancing was a form of training to quicken reflexes and develop parrying skills. Dancing in preparation for war was so common in Kongo that "dancing a war dance" (sanga-mento) was often used as a synonym for "to declare war" in seventeenth-century sources.[49]

Dancing was less useful in the period after 1680, since hand-to-hand combat was largely replaced by missile tactics with muskets. However, Africans did not use bayonets on their muskets; they needed swords and other hand-to-hand weapons for those times when close fighting was required. One Portuguese commander who fought in the late eighteenth century in southern Kongo, after praising his opponents' skill with muskets and their nearly universal use of the weapon, noted that they retained the "arma blanca" for hand-to-hand fighting.[50] Thus dancing may have been important even after guns became the principal weapons to ensure that soldiers still honed their skill in hand-to-hand fighting, or it may have survived just as close-order drill survives in modern armies, where it has little combat utility, as a distinctive element of military life. Luca da Caltanisetta still described the musketeer armies of the prince of Nsoyo in 1691 as dancing in preparation for war, and Castello de Vide noted dancing before battle in 1781.[51]

The African military background can also shed some light on the tactics of the Stono rebels. At first glance, they do not appear to have been very soldierly, standing in a disorderly group and dispersing after a brief engagement. Many rapidly fled to their masters' homes, and only a small determined core persisted, fighting several more encounters with the colonial militia in the days after the first battle.[52] It is most likely that, by the time the colonial forces met the rebels, their numbers had been swelled by a large number of slaves who had no military experience but hoped that the rebels would succeed and deliver them from slavery. When the real fighting began, these hangers-on might have been the ones who dispersed quickly, hoping to get back to their masters' farms before they were missed.[53]

But the tactics of the core of the rebels, perhaps those twenty Angolans who started the revolt and a few others, who had all the guns, disorderly as they seemed, are consistent with a central African model. Europeans' ideas of a proper military formation were based on the necessity, created by cavalry, of maintaining close order at all times. Indeed, the European musketeer of the eighteenth century was a converted pikeman, just as his musket with bayonet was a combination pike and missile weapon.[54] In central Africa, where there was never a large or effective cavalry, the musketeer was more likely to be a converted skirmisher. Central African musketeers in the seventeenth century often opened engagements with random fire from covered positions to weaken enemy infantry. This infantry was armed with swords and battle-axes intended for hand-to-hand fighting that would resolve the battle.[55] But, unlike Europeans, who retained the hand-to-hand aspects of pike warfare, central Africans greatly reduced their close fighting in favor of skirmishing tactics, which replaced the shock encounters of heavily armed infantry. Eighteenth-century battles tended to be drawn-out affairs in which units attacked the enemy, withdrew, maneuvered, and in general avoided hand-to-hand combat.[56]

Thus the Stono rebels were not revealing their rude origins when they fought in the way they did. Instead, their tactical behavior was perfectly consistent with tactics of the battlefields of Kongo. They withdrew after a brief encounter, relocated, and fought several battles over a protracted period, a pattern typical of Angola.

We can see the Stono Rebellion from a new angle if we consider the African contribution as well as the American one. The combination of evidence certainly suggests that the slaves' Christianity and the religious appeal of Spanish propaganda may have played a role in the revolt. Likewise, though less certain, the slaves' probable military experience in Africa could also have influenced their behavior and their ultimate fate.

## Notes

1. Peter H. Wood, *Black Majority: Negroes in Colonial South Carolina from 1670 through the Stono Rebellion* (New York: Knopf, 1974), pp. 56–62; Daniel Littlefield, *Rice and Slaves: Ethnicity and the Slave Trade in Colonial South Carolina* (Baton Rouge: Louisiana State University Press, 1981). I would like to thank the Carter Woodson Institute of the University of Virginia, whose support for the years 1984–1985 began the project from which this essay is drawn. I also benefited from a grant for additional research from the National Endowment for the Humanities, Summer Stipend (1988), on European military encounters with non-European Atlantic societies in the Columbian era. Finally, thanks to Joseph C. Miller, Linda M. Heywood, Michael Birkner, and Susan Mackielwicz for their comments on earlier versions.

2. Wood, *Black Majority,* pp. 63–91, 167–91.

3. Tom W. Shick, "Healing and Race in the South Carolina Low Country," in *Africans in Bondage: Studies in Slavery and the Slave Trade,* ed. Paul Lovejoy (Madison: University of Wisconsin Press, 1986), pp. 107–24; Margaret Washington Creel, *A Peculiar People: Slave Religion and Community-Culture among the Gullahs* (New York: New York University Press, 1988).

4. The problem is compounded by linguistic difficulties: to do historical studies of eighteenth-century Angola, the most important African source of slaves for South Carolina before Stono, one needs to consult sources written in Portuguese and Italian, very few of which are

available in translation and many of which are unpublished or have only been published in recent years.

5. See "An Account of the Negroe Insurrection in South Carolina" (undated, ca. 1740), in *Colonial Records of the State of Georgia*, ed. Allen D. Candler, Wm. J. Northern, and Lucian L. Knight (1904–1916; rept., New York: AMS, 1970), vol. 22, prt. 2, pp. 232–36. The most useful secondhand accounts are "A Ranger's Report of Travels with General Oglethorpe, 1739–1742," in *Travels in the American Colonies*, ed. Newton D. Mereness (New York: Macmillan, 1916), pp. 222–23; and William Stephens, *A Journal of the Proceedings in Georgia, Beginning October 24, 1737 . . .*, 2 vols. (London: Meadows, 1742), vol. 2, pp. 128–30 (this journal was also reprinted in *Colonial Records*, ed. Candler, Northern, and Knight, vol. 4). This last document is closest in time, dated September 13, 1739, just four days after the revolt.

6. Some of these events are reported in Stephens, *Journal*, vol. 2, pp. 77, 78. In retrospect, Stephens was glad that earlier they had stopped a priest on the Georgia coast (p. 130).

7. The earlier incidents are detailed in Wood, *Black Majority*, pp. 309–12; on runaways in Spanish Florida, see Jane Landers, "Gracia Real de Santa Teresa de Mose: A Free Black Town in Spanish Colonial Florida," *American Historical Review* 95 (February 1990): 9–30.

8. "Account of Negroe Insurrection," p. 233.

9. "Account of Negroe Insurrection," pp. 234–35; Stephens, *Journal*, p. 128.

10. Stephens, *Journal*, pp. 129, 235.

11. Andrew Leslie to Philip Bearcroft, January 7, 1740, quoted in Stephens, *Journal*, pp. 318–19; see also Frank J. Klingberg, *An Appraisal of the Negro in Colonial South Carolina: A Study in Americanization* (Washington, D.C.: Associated Publishers, 1941), p. 80.

12. Wood, *Black Majority*, pp. 271–320.

13. For a full discussion of the legal strictures as well as the substantial smuggling, see Joseph C. Miller, *Way of Death: Merchant Capitalism and the Angolan Slave Trade, 1730–1830* (Madison: University of Wisconsin Press, 1988), pp. 245–83.

14. A general survey of the English trade of this coast is presented in Phyllis M. Martin, *The External Trade of the Loango Coast, 1576–1870: The Effects of the Changing Commercial Relations on the Vili Kingdom of Loango* (Oxford: Clarendon Press, 1972), pp. 75–130.

15. David Galenson, *Traders, Planters, and Slaves: Market Behavior in Early English America* (Cambridge & New York: Cambridge University Press, 1986), pp. 164–65.

16. James Barbot, "Abstract of a Voyage to the Kongo River and Kabinda in 1700," in *A New General Collection of Voyages and Travels . . .*, 5 vols., ed. Thomas Astley (London: Astley, 1746), vol. 3, pp. 202–9.

17. Cherubino da Savona, "Breve ragguaglio del 'Regno di Congo, e sue Missione' scritto dal Padre Cerubino da Savona, Missionario Apostolico Capuccino" (MS of 1775), fols. 42, 44; mod. ed. in "Relazioni inedite di P. Cherubino Cassinis da Savona sul 'Congo e sue Missioni,'" ed. Carlo Toso, *L'Italiafrancescana* 45 (1975): 136–214. A French translation is available: Louis Jadin, "Aperçu de la situation du Congo en 1760 et rite d'élection des rois en 1775, d'après le P. Cherubino da Savona, missionaire au Congo de 1759 à 1774," *Bulletin, Institute historique belge de Rome* 35 (1963): 343–419.

18. For a detailed discussion on trading networks in Angola and its eastern regions, see Miller, *Way of Death*, pp. 207–83.

19. See Martin, *External Trade*, p. 130; Miller, *Way of Death*, pp. 200–203.

20. Miller, *Way of Death*, pp. 277–78, 582–85.

21. See, for example, Anselmo da Castelvetrano, "Relatione dello stato in cui presentmente si trovano le Missioni Cappuccini in Regno di Congo," October 14, 1742, Scritture riferite nel Congregazioni Generali, vol. 712, fols. 296–305, Archivio "De Propaganda Fide" (Rome). Also, ibid., Acta, vol. 112 (1742), fol. 422. On the general state of the Capuchin mission, and other ecclesiastical bodies in Kongo and Angola, see Graziano Saccardo [da Leguzzano], *Congo e Angola: Con la storia del missione dei Cappuccini*, 3 vols. (Venice: Curia provinciale dei Cappuccini,1982–1984), vol. 2, passim.

22. An extreme example comes from Kasanje in the 1660s; see Giovanni Antonio Cavazzi, "Missione Evangelica al Regno di Congo" (MS of 1665), Book 3, MSS Araldi Family (Modena).

23. Beatrix Heintze, "Luso-African Feudalism in Angola? The Vassal Treaties of the Sixteenth to Eighteenth Centuries," *Revista Portuguesa de História* 18 (1980): 111–31.

24. Da Savona, "Breve ragguaglio," fol. 42.

25. Documents cited and quoted in Jorge Palacios Preciado, *La Trata de negros por Cartagena de Indias* (Tunja: Universidad Pedagógica y Tecnológica Colombia, 1973), p. 349.

26. John K. Thornton, "Demography and History in the Kingdom of Kongo, 1550–1750," *Journal of African History* 18 (1977): 507–30.

27. For the origin and development of Christianity in Kongo, see Thornton, "The Development of an African Catholic Church in the Kingdom of Kongo, 1491–1750," *Journal of African History* 25 (1984): 147–49.

28. Anne Hilton, *The Kingdom of Kongo* (Oxford: Clarendon Press / New York: Oxford University Press, 1985), pp. 179–98; Wyatt MacGaffey, *Religion and Society in Central Africa: The Bakongo of Lower Zaire* (Chicago: University of Chicago Press, 1986), pp. 198–211; Andrea da Pavia, "Viaggio Apostolico alla Missione" (MS ca. 1690), MS 3165, Biblioteca Nacional de Madrid; da Savona, "Breve ragguaglio," passim; Rafael Castello de Vide, "Viagem do Congo do Missionário Fr. Raphael de Castello de Vide, hoje Bispo do São Tomé" (MS of 1788), MS Vermelho, 296 fol. 77 and passim, Academia das Cienças (Lisbon).

29. For example, see the account of da Savona, "Breve ragguaglio," fols. 42v, 43, 45, 45v. Also see, Castello de Vide, "Viagem do Congo," fols. 53, 64, and passim.

30. François Bontinck, "Les Croix du bois dans l'ancien royaume de Kongo," *Miscellanea historiae pontificiae* 50 (1983): 199–213.

31. In addition to the correspondence of Antonio de Salas cited above, see Thornton, "On the Trail of Voodoo: African Christianity in Africa and the Americas," *The Americas* 44 (1988): 268–69.

32. Landers, "Gracia Real de Santa Teresa de Mose," p. 27, citing a baptismal register entry of January 26, 1748. The catechism text was reprinted with French translation and annotation by Bontinck and D. Ndembe Nsasi, *Le Catéchisme kikongo de 1624: Reédition critique* (Brussels: Koninklijke Academie voor Overzeese Wetenschappen, 1978). Italian clergy introduced a new edition in 1650, and copies were extant in the nineteenth century.

33. See Rui da Pina's untitled account (in an early-sixteenth-century Italian translation), fol. 99rb–100vb, photographically reproduced in Francisco Leite da Faria, "Uma relação de Rui de Pina sobre o Congo escrita em 1492," *Studia* 19 (1966), which quotes a letter of the king of Kongo written about September or October 1491. The author of the letter is likely to have been a Kongolese who had visited Portugal between 1488 and 1491, "a black Christian who knew

how to read and write, who began to teach the young men (moços) of the Court and children of the nobility, which is a great number"; Rui da Pina, Cronica del Rey D. Joham I (ca. 1515), cap. 63, excerpted in Monumenta Missionaria Africana: Africa occidental, 1st ser., 14 vols., ed. António Brásio (Lisbon: Agência Geral do Ultramar, Divisão de Publicações e Biblioteca, 1952–1981), vol. 1, p. 136.

34. For a summary of Capuchin educational work, see Saccardo [da Leguzzano], Congo e Angola, vol. 1, pp. 402–15.

35. On literacy, see Thornton, The Kingdom of Kongo: Civil War and Transition, 1641–1718 (Madison: University of Wisconsin Press, 1983), pp. 67–68; Hilton, Kingdom of Kongo, pp. 79–83, 205, 217; Susan H. Broadhead, "Beyond Decline: The Kingdom of the Kongo in the Eighteenth and Nineteenth Centuries," International Journal of African Historical Studies 12 (1979): 633–35.

36. Jean-Luc Vellut, "Relations internationales au moyen-Kwango et d'Angola dans la deuxième moitié du XVIIIe siècle," Études d'histoire africaine 1 (1970): 82–89.

37. This was a constant complaint of mid-eighteenth-century governors; see, for example, Memorial of Francisco Innocencio de Sousa Coutinho, 1765, Fundo Geral, Códice 8554, fol. 28, Biblioteca Nacional de Lisboa. This and other complaints ought to be taken as indications of the failure of the Portuguese government to replace Kimbundu as the language of the colony, rather than that Portuguese was not known. Sousa Coutinho took Brazil, a completely Lusophonic country (in his opinion), as a model.

38. This use had religious implications; see Thornton, "On the Trail of Voodoo," pp. 271–73.

39. Wood, Black Majority, p. 127.

40. Wood proposes that African soldiers may have been brought to the Americas and cited the use of firearms in Africa, although the evidence relates to the Gold Coast rather than Angola (ibid., pp. 126–27).

41. Thornton, Kingdom of Kongo, pp. xiv–xv. Slaves in the New World known as "Congos" were typically transshipped through the country from farther east and exported either through Kongo ports or by Angola-based merchants who crossed Kongo to buy slaves.

42. Angelo Maria da Polinago to Dorotea Sofia di Neoburgo, August 16, 1733, Raccolta manuscritti, busta 49, Viaggi, fol. 3, Archivio di Stato, Parma.

43. "Account of Negroe Insurrection," p. 233.

44. Thornton, Kingdom of Kongo, p. 42.

45. Tomassi da Cortona to Anibal Tomassi, November 20, 1734, Tomassi Papers, fol. 2; Angelo Maria da Polinago to Dorotea Sofia di Neoburgo, August 16, 1733, Raccolta manoscritti, busta 49, Viaggi, fol. 2, Archivio di Stato, Parma.

46. Miller has argued that firearms were less important in central Africa than proposed here. His main basis for this is the conclusion that firearms imports were insufficient to arm more than about 20,000 soldiers in the whole of central Africa (Way of Death, pp. 86–94), even though he estimates that as many as 60,000 guns were imported per year. This low number derives from a pessimistic judgment of the capacity of Africans to repair defective imports or maintain existing weapons. I believe Miller is wrong in part because of the eyewitness evidence of large armies armed with muskets cited in previous notes and also on the grounds that his estimates of imports, number of serviceable weapons at any time, repair capacities of African smiths, and average life span of weapons are all considerably too low.

47. "Account of Negroe Insurrection," p. 234. Wood proposes a religious interpretation for the banners (*Black Majority*, p. 316, n. 30), even though no eighteenth-century source mentions the sort of cultic devotion to flags that he suggests. Unit flags were commonplace, however, in seventeenth-century armies; see Thornton, "The Art of War in Angola, 1575–1680," *Comparative Studies in Society and History* 30 (April 1988): 360–78 (esp. 366–67); and Castello de Vide mentions them as always being a part of any force in the later eighteenth century (de Vide, "Viagem do Congo," fols. 93, 96).

48. "Account of Negroe Insurrection," p. 234.

49. It is so used, for the seventeenth century, even in sources by Europeans; see Mateus Cardoso, "Relação do alevamento de Dom Afonso, irmão del Rey Dom Alvaro III de Congo" (January 1622), Assistencia Portugal, vol. 55, fol. 115v, Archivum Romanum Societatis Iesu (Rome).

50. Paulo Martins Pinheiro de Lacerda, "Noticia da campanha e paiz do Mosul, que conquistou o Sargento Mor Paulo Martins Pinheiro de Lacerda" (1790–1791), *Annaes Maritímos e Colonais* 6 (1846): 129–30. Miller (*Way of Death*, p. 91, n. 57), cites this account as evidence that the Kongo possessed few guns and still fought with their traditional weapons. In fact, he pointedly praises their skill with firearms in a way that suggests it was their principal weapon, noting the use of the "arma blanca" as a secondary weapon. The use of musket fire is also clear in other accounts by Pinheiro de Lacerda, which describe the actual battles of the same campaign in greater detail; see Angola, Caixa 76, doc. 28 (May 20, 1791), Arquivo Histórico Ultramarino (Lisbon); and doc. 34, service record of Felix Xavier Pinheiro de Lacerda (his son), enclosure by Paulo Martins Pinheiro de Lacerda.

51. Luca da Caltanisetta, "Relatione del viaggo e missione fatta per me fra' Luca da Caltanissetta . . . nel 1691 al . . . ," (MS of 1701), fols. 9, 25v published in Romain Romero, ed., *Il Congo agli inizi del settecento nella relazione di p. Luca da Caltanissetta* (Florence: La nuova Italia, 1974?); Castello de Vide, "Viagem do Congo," MS Vermelho 296, fols. 98, 119, Academia das Cienças. He also witnessed a *sangamento* in a village, which he compares to these military dances, and was told that the people were in fact dancing to make war on the Devil (fol. 137).

52. Documents summarized in Wood, *Black Majority*, pp. 318–20.

53. "Account of Negroe Insurrection," p. 235.

54. William H. McNeill, *The Pursuit of Power: Technology, Armed Force, and Society since 1000* (Chicago: University of Chicago Press, 1982), pp. 125–39. When fighting with Native Americans, and even during the colonial wars, colonial militias sometimes abandoned these principles, however, much to the chagrin of their professional leaders or opponents.

55. Thornton, "Art of War," pp. 363, 374.

56. The best description involves a southern Kongo army fighting Portuguese-led forces in the eighteenth century; Elias Alexandre da Silva Corrêa, *História de Angola*, 2 vols. (Lisbon: Atica, 1937), vol. 2, pp. 48–62. See the interesting description of tactics in Pinheiro de Lacerda, "Noticia da campanha," pp. 131–32.

Essay 3

# Rebelling as Men

## Edward A. Pearson

Edward A. Pearson's careful and thoughtful essay reevaluates the rebellion by examining the gendered division of labor among lowcountry slaves. Pearson, who teaches at Franklin and Marshall College, explains the Stono revolt by placing it within the larger context of the lowcountry's economic and cultural transformation. Specifically, he considers how the lowcountry's shift from a frontier to a plantation society changed gender relations, which in turn shaped the contours of the revolt at Stono.

---

Despite the dearth of sources, the Stono insurrection has attracted the attention of a number of historians.[1] Alexander Hewatt, author of the colony's first history, suggested that, had the rebels not been defeated, the entire lowcountry would "have fallen sacrifice to their great power and indiscriminate fury."[2] In his now-classic account of lowcountry slave culture, Peter Wood devotes much attention to the uprising, concluding that the significant rise of slaves directly from Africa combined with formal and informal restrictions against this growing slave population provided a context for rebellion.[3] For Wood, Stono acts as a watershed in the lowcountry's history, demarcating a period of racial fluidity associated with frontier life from the severity and discipline of plantation agriculture. Some scholars, however, do not regard the rebellion as the pivotal moment in the history of slavery in the lowcountry. Both Michael Mullin and M. Eugene Sirmans disagree with the importance that Wood accords the rising, arguing it was "less an insurrection than an attempt by slaves to fight their way to St. Augustine."[4] Others have used it to explore additional facets of slave society. John Thornton has compared how Kongolese military skills shaped the organization and tactics of the Stono rebels, concluding that ethnic martial traditions had a profound influence on their conduct and the final outcome of the rising.[5]

Source: Edward A. Pearson, "'A Countryside Full of Flames': A Reconsideration of the Stono Rebellion and Slave Rebelliousness in the Early Eighteenth-Century South Carolina Lowcountry," *Slavery and Abolition* 17, no. 2 (1996): 22–50. The edited version of the essay that appears here is reprinted by permission the author and of Taylor & Francis, Ltd., U.K. http://www.tandf.co.uk/journals.

Building on these contributions, this essay offers a reappraisal of the rebellion by considering the role that the gendered division of labor may have played in the creation of lowcountry slave culture and the uprising itself. Gender, as Joan Scott has observed, offers a useful analytical tool that allows historians to explore how appropriate roles for women and men are socially constructed and the ways in which different societies ascribe value to certain activities according to the organization of labor along lines of sex.[6] I wish to suggest here that the transformation of the lowcountry's agricultural economy from a frontier to a plantation society may have had a dramatic impact on gender relations and that this rebellion can be understood in gendered terms as a moment in which enslaved African men articulated their masculinity. It should be noted, however, that as neither travelers, colonial officials, nor planters directly addressed the gendered organization of labor on rice estates, the following discussion offers speculative rather than definitive conclusions.

Before the rice revolution of the early eighteenth century transformed the lowcountry's economy, a large number of male slaves experienced some degree of autonomy as cattle herders or foresters in their daily lives.[7] The rise of large-scale rice cultivation demanded that the organization of agricultural work be reconfigured. In addition to imposing a routinized work regime in the rice fields, planters used male slaves to grow and harvest this crop. By so doing, they violated the sexual division of labor that had customarily structured agricultural labor in the societies of western and west-central Africa from which a significant number of slaves who worked on lowcountry plantations originated. By transgressing the definitions of appropriate gender roles that prevailed in Atlantic Africa in the workplace, lowcountry plantation owners may have galvanized male slaves to rebel against the social and cultural consequences of the rice revolution that swept across coastal Carolina in the early 1700s. I want to suggest, moreover, that the consequences of the rice revolution and the sexual organization of plantation work may be discerned in events surrounding the Stono uprising. [. . .]

For several decades after its establishment by English and Afro-Barbadian pioneers in 1670, South Carolina remained, as Russell Menard has recently noted, "a struggling, unimpressive, outpost colony."[8] In addition to an indigenous population of some 7,500, the lowcountry was peopled by about 3,260 whites and 2,444 slaves by 1700 who depended primarily on subsistence farming, pastoral agriculture, and the provisions trade (naval supplies, deerskins, and dried goods) for their livelihoods.[9] As the backbone of the labor force, African and Afro-Caribbean slaves worked as cattle herders and foresters as well as field hands as their owners sought to discover a staple that would yield profits as large as those reaped by Caribbean sugar planters. [. . .]

For the slaves who worked along the cattle frontier, gender played a primary role in the configuration of labor. Research by John Otto and Peter Wood has indicated that cattle ranchers used slave men as ranch hands. John Smyth, for example, owned fifty-three cattle that were tended by three white male servants and three slave men; James Joyner's three male slaves supervised a herd of some two hundred animals; and Bernard Schenkingh's holdings on James Island included "134 Head of Cattle [and] One Negro Man."[10] After completing his indenture in 1672, Dennis Mahone became a small independent farmer who, after speculating in land and cattle with some success, sold "fower calves & three steers, five sows and one boare & a negro man named Cato" to a new settler in 1681.[11] A sizeable number of slave men appear to have spent their working lives in the lowcountry's forests and on its savannas, herding cattle and hogs. Moreover, as many early settlers appear not to have held title to the land on which they grazed their animals, their cattle doubtless roamed freely across the "thriving Range" of the coastal plain.[12] These slaves likely experienced a moderate degree of geographic mobility and modest levels of independence as they supervised the herds and built the wooden pens in which to house the animals against the appetites of "the Tygar, Wolf and Wild Catt" that also roamed the region.[13] Unlike the discipline that would characterize plantation work, the semi-nomadic character of ranching resulted in greater autonomy for enslaved men. Lacking the acreage necessary for grazing cattle, most ranchers let their animals graze and forage "wild in the woods."[14] To prevent cattle from falling prey to predators and becoming feral, slave herdsmen would round up the herds at nightfall, blowing horns and luring them into the corral "with a little Indian corn . . . Turnips and other roots."[15] This daily routine would be punctuated by other tasks associated with pastoral agriculture. After the spring calving, herdsmen would "ride out in search for them in the woods," returning the new animals to the cattle pens for branding.[16] In addition, slaves would maintain the pens, repairing gates and fences, as well as drive the animals to market.

The flexible routines of pastoral agriculture allowed these slaves to pursue a number of activities independent of their primary job. Apart from supervising calving early in the year and driving cattle to market in the fall, pastoralism did not place severe demands on their time.[17] At the center of their lives stood the cattle pen itself. Often situated some distance from the "Neighbourhood of Planters," these small settlements usually consisted of provision grounds, several buildings to house both animals and people and the pens themselves.[18] [. . .] In addition to their duties as herdsmen, male slaves likely hunted, taking advantage of the lowcountry's abundance of wild animals and fish. These activities may have made the pens virtually self-sufficient, perhaps reinforcing the sensation of autonomy that slaves may have experienced as frontier herders.[19] [. . .] In the pens' ramshackle huts, slaves perhaps fashioned a congenial setting in which to exchange news, tell tales, and consume meals from the commodities that surrounded them. The long process of shaping some sense of community among lowcountry slaves may have started in the cattle pens dotted about the coastal lowlands.

In contrast, the small population of slave women (estimated at around 1,100 in the late seventeenth century) worked at a range of agricultural and domestic tasks that kept them within the farm or cattle pen. One promotional tract suggested that they cultivated the small kitchen gardens that surrounded the pens. In addition, female slaves also performed tasks associated with animal husbandry, including milking, churning butter, and making cheese.[20] This labor arrangement conformed to the broad pattern of female work in western Africa, where women did domestic work, gathering water and fuel, preparing and processing food, and raising children. Not only did enslaved women supervise the slave household as plantation agriculture came to the lowcountry, but their domestic role expanded to include the marketing of goods grown on their own provision grounds in Charles Town's markets.

Pastoral agriculture, moreover, demanded the acquisition and application of a number of skills associated with livestock management. If they had not mastered the skill already, slaves likely learned how to ride and maintain horses. [. . .] The local knowledge that they gained may have been put to use later as some slaves established temporary maroon camps or planned escapes from South Carolina to Spanish Florida. As a vital and early form of agricultural labor that depended on enslaved Africans, the practice of pastoralism perhaps established the foundation upon which rural slaves in the lowcountry fashioned their culture. [. . .]

The working environment in which these pioneer slaves found themselves bore a number of similarities to that which prevailed in West Africa. The division of labor by sex was fundamental to economic and social life in both locales.[21] Men and women worked to meet the obligations of running their households, but the way they allocated their labor differed from that of their European counterparts. In observing how villagers on the Guinea coast ran their households, English traders and travelers, who wrote from the perspective of a society in which the association of female work with domestic tasks rendered it far less visible than men's labor, noted the significant amount of agricultural and domestic work African women performed. Traveling through Dahomey in the mid-eighteenth century, slave trader Robert Norris observed Yoruba women "tilling the ground . . . they were also occupied in spinning cotton, weaving clothes, and brewing pitto [beer], in dressing victuals for sale, and carrying merchandises to market."[22] This organization of work prevailed elsewhere in Atlantic Africa.[23] To the south, Girolama Merolla, a missionary in the Kongo, observed how men constructed houses and cared for trees that yielded cloth, utensils, medicines, and palm wine while women provided food for both use at home and sale in local markets.[24] Women generally spent their days "in a continual state of employment" as they worked in the field and house while men were engaged in other tasks to complement these activities.[25]

For a significant number of men along the Guinea coast, pastoral agriculture was central to the village economy. A task that often removed them from the vicinity of the village, herding demanded that men travel long distances in search of grazing and water along the Senegal and Gambia River valleys.[26] Men did perform work associated with certain aspects of arable farming, but the accounts of a number of travelers suggest that just as many African males were involved in other agricultural pursuits that did not conform to the organization of labor on English farms. This attitude perhaps prompted at least one English trader to observe how "men for their parts do lead an idle kind of life."[27] For these pastoralists, however, life was anything but idle as they cared for the animals that constituted an important part of their wealth.[28]

The social organization of labor for men in the societies of western and west-central Africa bore similarities to the ways in which ranchers arranged work on the lowcountry frontier. Among the ethnic groups who lived along the Upper Guinea coast, cattle played a vital role in the domestic and commercial economies of peoples like the Balantas, Djolas, and Wolof. Around Cape Verde, French trader Jean Barbot observed how the traffic in cattle between the Wolof and people from the interior, possibly the nomadic Fulani who grazed their herds across the vastness of the western Sudan, stimulated a flourishing trade in hides.[29] Using techniques that would become familiar in the lowcountry, these herders would pasture the animals during the day and enclose them at night "in pens formed in clearings . . . closed round with a fence of thorns and briars."[30] These pens of Upper Guinea may have been the antecedents for those constructed by lowcountry slaves. [. . .]

The similarities between the male work culture of herding [. . .] in Atlantic Africa and these pursuits in South Carolina had implications for slave life in the eighteenth-century lowcountry. The Afro-Caribbean slaves who initially peopled the frontier may have experienced enough independence for them to replicate certain aspects of the work culture of their native societies. Perhaps working at tasks with which they were familiar helped to vitiate the dishonor and degradation that played a central part in the psychology of domination and enslavement.[31] For slaves from the Caribbean, the fluid work arrangements of the frontier stood in stark contrast to the rigidities of the sugar-plantation regime. Moreover, as many of these Caribbean imports originated from these same regions of West Africa, a return to the more familiar world of pastoral and arboreal agriculture may have fostered some sense of self-worth and restored some measure of dignity to lowcountry slaves.[32] This frontier world, however, was about to undergo profound changes as rice emerged as the colony's premier cash crop.[33]

The shift in the economy from ranching and lumbering to rice brought about a dramatic change in the ethnic composition of the slave population in the lowcountry. Slaves from the Caribbean no longer dominated the Charles Town market as rice planters began strengthening their ties to the Atlantic traders by purchasing laborers with some familiarity with rice cultivation in the early eighteenth century.[34] Some 257 slaves (44 percent) out of the 582 slaves brought into the colony in 1717 came from Guinea, while 217 (37 percent) came from the Caribbean. By the next year, the difference in the origins of imports from these two regions had grown significantly, with 74 percent of slaves arriving in Charles Town originating from the Guinea coast.[35] This shift began the long process of the Africanization of the low-country's enslaved labor force as imports from Atlantic Africa first supplemented then supplanted Afro-Caribbean slaves.[36]

The provenance of African slave imports gradually shifted at the start of the eighteenth century. Ships carrying slaves from the rice-growing regions of the Senegambia and the Gulf of Guinea continued to arrive throughout the 1720s. As Daniel Littlefield has shown, these slaves were highly sought after by lowcountry planters.[37] By the 1730s, however, these planters also began buying slaves from British merchants who were active along the Loango coast of west-central Africa and were purchasing slaves from the kingdom of Kongo and Angola.[38] Of the 10,661 slaves imported between 1735 and 1739, traders designated 6,310 (59 percent) as Angolan; the remainder were listed as African (3,585, or 34 percent), Gambian (615, or 6 percent), or Caribbean (133, or 1 percent). In 1738, the year before the rebellion, some 1,462 slaves landed in South Carolina, of which 906 slaves (62 percent) were listed as from west-central Africa, with the remainder being from Africa (28.5 percent), the Gambia (8.5 percent), or the Caribbean (1 percent).[39] Although traders sold enslaved women and children, the correspondence of merchants like Henry Laurens and John Guerard as well as auction notices indicate that planters preferred young adult slave men over slave women. For the South Carolina trade, notes David Richardson, "these age and sex preferences were not unusual: on the contrary, they were fairly typical of planter preferences throughout British America before the Revolution."[40] Such patterns are entirely consistent with the Atlantic trade, in which 179 male slaves were exported for every 100 enslaved women.[41]

Between 1670 and the late 1730s, the colony experienced three overlapping waves of slave importation. African and Afro-Caribbean slaves preceded slaves from the Senegambia and Gulf of Guinea, who were, in turn, followed by captives from west-central Africa. As the first coerced laborers in the colony, Afro-Caribbean slaves constituted a "charter group," able to create their own folkways from a combination of their own traditions and the circumstances of frontier life as well as to establish boundaries for the incorporation of newcomers.[42] The new imports from Guinea and the Senegambia encountered a society in which the basic contours for cultural innovation among slaves had already been broadly defined. As Sidney Mintz and Richard Price have noted on this aspect of slave culture, the arrival of "massive new importations from Africa apparently had little more effect than to lead to secondary elaborations."[43]

This is not to say that newcomers to lowcountry plantations had no impact on the process of cultural formation in the slave quarters. The final wave of slaves from Kongo and Angola appear to have enjoyed several advantages over those taken from western Africa. Unlike slaves from the Senegambia and the Gulf of Guinea, where the heterogeneous cultures of the region's numerous ethnic groups did not facilitate the making of broad cultural commonalities, these new arrivals from west-central Africa came from remarkably homogenous societies. Drawn together by the common lexical base of Bantu languages, these people had also experienced some contact with Portuguese traders and Jesuit and Capuchin missionaries.[44]

Of the slaves taken from this region of Africa, it is likely that some were familiar with Roman Catholicism, even though Kongo Christianity was highly syncretic in nature, and some may have had some ability in either Italian, the language of the Capuchins, or Portuguese. Moreover, some slaves may have also had an acquaintance with English after the Royal African Company established trading posts along the Loango coast at Malimba and Kabinda, competing with its European rivals for trade at the turn of the eighteenth century.[45] This region subsequently became a major source of slaves for English possessions in the New World, with over 20 percent of its imports coming from the lands between the Zaire River and Gabon Estuary. Many of these captives were young adult males; it was here, according to Paul Lovejoy, that "the goal of purchasing twice as many males as females appears to have been realized for the first time."[46] Like so many other prisoners of war in Atlantic Africa, a significant number of these men would have been soldiers who, on becoming captives of their enemies, were sold into slavery.[47] Both language and military skills, as we shall later see, would play major parts in the rebellion of 1739. [. . .]

Throughout the 1730s, planters continued to expand the commercial production of rice on estates laboriously carved from swamps and creeks by slaves.[48] Rice exports underwent explosive growth, rising from six hundred to ten thousand tons between 1709 and 1731, an average increase of 20 percent per annum.[49] The low-country also underwent a demographic revolution as the number of slaves rose from 5,768 to around 20,000 over the same period.[50] Already a society dependent on slave labor prior to the commercial cultivation of rice, South Carolina was transformed into a plantation society.

That a large number of lowcountry slaves came from regions in which rice was grown and that these captives were preferred by planters has been documented by Daniel Littlefield, Peter Wood and others.[51] The role played by women in its production has not received as much attention, however. A major staple throughout the Senegambia and, to a lesser degree, along the Grain, Ivory, Gold, and Slave Coasts of the Gulf of Guinea, the crop was almost universally cultivated by women.[52] Trading with the Mende along the Sherbro coast of the Senegambia in the 1730s and 1740s, Irish trader Nicholas Owens saw women "making plantations and beating out the rice."[53] In his account of its cultivation among the Baga, Capt. Samuel Gamble, who also traded in this region, observed how "Women & Girls transplant the rice and are so dextrous as to plant fifty roots in a minute" and detailed the manner by which they cultivated and harvested the crop.[54] Other traders and naval officers concurred with these observations: Thomas Winterbottom, a navy surgeon, noted that they "not only cook, and wash and beat the rice, clean it from the husk, but they also cut down the under wood, assist in hoeing the ground, and they carry the produce to market."[55] This grain, however, was not widely cultivated in either the Kongo or Angola. According to one traveler, rice was "little thought of" and mainly used to provision slave ships.[56] Whatever crop was being grown, women rather than men played the central role in its cultivation in Atlantic Africa.

To meet the demands of rice cultivation, planters dissolved the gender division of labor that had characterized slave work along the ranching and lumbering frontier. The new configuration of work combined the imposition of the disciplined work routine of plantation cultivation with the violation of western African constructions of appropriate gender roles for agricultural work. Thomas Nairne, a planter from St. Helena Parish, demanded that "slaves of both Sexes" labor in his fields, while pastor Johann Martin Bolzius noted that slaves, regardless of their sex, were required to cultivate a certain acreage of land per day.[57] As rice fields and irrigation channels transformed the lowland countryside, both male and female slaves found themselves working side by side. This arrangement violated the cornerstone of the economic and social organization of village culture in western Africa. Already dishonored by their status as captives, these new arrivals perhaps suffered another insult to their honor by having to perform tasks traditionally done by women. [. . .]

The changes that rice cultivation brought to the lowcountry furnished the context in which the revolt occurred. Many slaves may have been only partly aware of the region's changing ethnic and demographic patterns, but they would have been very conscious of how rice cultivation was reshaping their working lives. The backbreaking nature of this work, combined with the transgression of gender roles that had prevailed in Atlantic Africa, gave male slaves a specific set of grievances against which to struggle.[58]

The 1730s was a decade of slave unrest throughout the New World plantation complex. Conspiracies were uncovered in the Bahamas in 1734 and in Antigua a year later, while war between colonists and maroons broke out on Jamaica in 1730, and rebellions occurred on Saint John in 1733 and on Guadalupe in 1737.[59] Part of the Atlantic system, South Carolina likewise experienced unrest and discontent among its slave population as well as military threats from the Spanish. [. . .]

Between 1732 and 1739, the *South Carolina Gazette* reported that 253 slaves had escaped slavery. Even though they constitute the tip of "an otherwise indeterminate iceberg," these notices offer a rough profile of individuals who successfully "stole themselves."[60] As in every slave regime, male slaves comprised the majority of lowcountry fugitives, making up 77 percent (or 194 slaves).[61] Over three-quarters of these men lived in the countryside and departed at the most arduous times of rice cultivation in January and February, when they had to clean ditches and prepare fields, and in September and October, when they worked long hours reaping, transporting, and threshing the harvest. Perhaps it is no accident that rebellion occurred as plantation work reached its most intense and when slave men, reaping a bumper rice harvest in 1739, may have been provoked to contemplate flight.

The African origins of the advertised runaways provides further information on the relationship between resistance and ethnicity.[62] Although the provenance of some Stono rebels suggests that recently arrived African men were more likely to oppose slavery, we cannot definitively conclude that African-born slaves were more prone to escape than their American-born counterparts because information on ethnicity is often absent from the notices. Between 1732 and 1739, however, the available evidence indicates that enslaved Africans, who constituted the bulk of lowcountry slaves by the 1730s, also made up the majority of fugitives. Out of 192 men who ran, the paper reported 62 slaves (32 percent) as being African (with 26, or 13 percent, of these being Angolan) and 17 (or 8 percent) as being either native-born or from the Caribbean. Among the remaining 87 slaves (45 percent), it is very probable that some were non-native born slaves.[63] In these eight years, therefore, 46 percent of all male escapees came from some part of Atlantic Africa. What we know about the ethnicity of the rebels and their leader indicates that they came from Angola, but this does not preclude either slaves from other parts of Atlantic Africa or even the "country born" from being among their ranks.[64]

In addition to growing problems in Anglo-Spanish relations and the presence of an increasingly restive slave population, the combination of bad weather and disease further added to the problems faced by the colonists. Torrential rains in the summer of 1737 contributed to poor harvests of rice and other staples, leading to a "Great Scarcity of Corn, Pease, Small Rice, Flower and Bisket" and contributing to the death of some slaves from "want."[65] Although there was a poor harvest next year, it did not lead to any deaths. It was a smallpox epidemic that proved to be the killer in 1738, spreading throughout Charles Town and some rural areas during the summer and autumn months and leaving several hundred people, slave and free, dead. As the colony recovered from this outbreak, yellow fever erupted the following summer, leaving the colony in "a deplorable state" in the closing months of the year.[66] Trade came to a virtual standstill, the Assembly removed itself from Charles Town for its sessions, the South Carolina Gazette closed temporarily, and as the first week of September ended, reports about the outbreak of hostilities between Spain and England arrived.[67] The continual traffic between the town and its hinterlands ensured that the trials besetting the colony would spread throughout the lowcountry.

The presence of epidemic disease and food shortages and the threat of attacks by the Spanish had an impact on enslaved as well as free people. For slaves, the possibility of war meant a further imposition on their freedom of movement as Gov.

Thomas Broughton, having informed imperial officials that "our Negroes are . . . and more dreadfull to our safety than any Spanish invaders," doubled the number and strength of patrols and used Cherokee Indians to shore up the colony's internal security.[68] In addition to these patrols, scout boats stationed along the coast further impeded slave self-activity. Some lowcountry slaves may have interpreted the militia's presence along with the other misfortunes as portents of some undefined event of great magnitude. Others may have recognized that preparations for war signaled the start of a major challenge by the Spanish to English mastery in the region. Whether these slaves saw the soldiers at St. Augustine as an army of liberation is unknown, but these menacing events may have been perceived as heralding a moment of impending yet unknown change.[69]

The tocsin of rebellion rang in the early hours of Sunday morning on 9 September as rebellious slaves assembled outside Hutchenson's store under Jemmy's leadership. Jemmy is described only as "their Captain" and an Angolan; we know nothing else about the man. That no other rebel was individually identified perhaps indicates that he held a position of prominence on a plantation or among local slaves. Whatever his place in the community, he may have visited nearby estates to recruit slaves. Although Bull alluded to it thirty years after the insurrection, the role that "work on the public road," a task in which a number of rebels were apparently involved over the course of several days, played in the insurrection is worth considering.[70] Drawn from several local plantations and farms, the members of the road gang likely exchanged the laborious work of the rice harvest for the equally arduous labor of road work. Moreover, as these workers would have been male, Jemmy perhaps took advantage of the overseer's slack inspection to convince his fellow workers to rebel.[71]

But did Jemmy intend to launch a full-scale rebellion or did he plan to escape with a number of other slaves? Jemmy may have aimed to lead some slaves across coastal Carolina and Georgia to St. Augustine. They may have intended to take supplies from Hutchenson's store and then effect their escape as the colonists prepared themselves for attack by Spanish forces.[72] By starting their action on Sunday, when many white people would have been at worship and when planters allowed slaves "to work for themselves" on their provision grounds, the rebels would have been able to take advantage of a day when their masters may have been less vigilant and other enslaved people were engaged in their own unsupervised affairs. After the killings at the store, the slaves perhaps decided to fight their way to freedom. The rebels alternatively may have intended to inflict as much damage as possible on their owners and their property before striking south toward the promise of liberation.

Whatever their original intention, the slaves transformed themselves from field hands into rebels in that moment of drama and violence at Hutchenson's store. Perhaps it was a moment in which they recovered a sense of martial identity that may have informed many of their lives in Africa. These killings and the display of the severed heads of Bathurst and Gibbs on the steps served as a public declaration. From a practical standpoint, the raid furnished the rebels with the arms and ammunition necessary to conduct a successful rising. Their actions at the store spoke not just to pragmatic concerns, however. They also illuminated the consciousness of the insurgents. The murder and subsequent decapitation of the two men in the store indicate the presence of violent rage, but these acts likely also possessed some symbolic content for the rebels.

Through the ritual brutalization of these men, the rebels were able to invert the power relations in which they found themselves embedded. The very act of rebellion itself clearly threatened to turn the world upside down, but decapitation may have had a specific meaning for the rebels.[73] Often an integral part to the punishment that colonial authorities inflicted on slaves found guilty of serious offences, beheading was performed as a public spectacle. Both free and slave inhabitants of Charles Town saw the execution of a man named Quash for burglary in 1734. After the hanging his "Head was sever'd from his Body, and fixed upon the Gallows."[74] A few months before the rising, the bodies of two executed slaves were "hung in Chains by Hang Man's Point . . . in sight of all negroes passing and repassing by water."[75] Away from the courtroom, slaveholders also occasionally administered this brand of justice. After killing an escaped slave in early 1732, Charles Jones was ordered by a judge to remove the head, "fix it on a pole and set it near the crossroads."[76] Reports of these executions no doubt reached slaves on lowcountry plantations. Appropriating this form of punishment for themselves, the rebels inverted patterns of discipline used by the authorities for their own purposes.

This incident may have held yet another symbolic meaning for the rebels. Decapitation not only played a part in the exercise of colonial justice; it was also integral to the martial culture of several western African societies. Robin Law has noted how warriors in Dahomey and neighboring areas beheaded their enemies, displaying the severed heads as trophies of military prowess and preserving them for ritual display.[77] An English slave trader at Whydah on the Bight of Benin watched soldiers "return from ravaging" carrying "bags full of men, women, and childrens heads" into the royal compound, which they proceeded to "kick and sling about" with great energy.[78] By beheading the men and displaying their heads, the rebels may have been participating in a time-honored tradition firmly grounded in their own martial culture.

After declaring their intent at the Stono Bridge, the rebels headed down the Pon Pon road and into the heart of St. Paul's Parish. As they marched through the countryside, they continued on their course of violence. After plundering the house of the Godfrey family and killing its inhabitants, they reached Wallace's Tavern and the Lemy house by daybreak. Instead of destroying both buildings and their residents, the insurgents elected to save the tavern keeper, who was "a Good Man and kind to his Slaves," and kill Lemy, his wife, and child.[79] The nature of Wallace's benevolence toward his slaves remains a mystery, but as a tavern keeper he may have broken the law, served alcohol to slaves, and tacitly encouraged them to patronize his establishment in exchange for goods. Their decision to kill Lemy's family and spare Wallace's suggests the ways in which the rebels calculated the value of the people who had once presided over their lives. [. . .]

The incidents that transpired at the house inhabited by Thomas Rose reveal the ambiguous character of solidarity and community among lowcountry slaves. Rather than join the rebels, Rose's slave hid his master before stepping outside to pacify the rebels.[80] This slave was not alone in selecting this course of action. Several slaves owned by Thomas Elliott followed this example, demonstrating "Integrity and Fidelity" to their owner rather than to their potential liberators.[81] For July, another of Elliott's slaves, this display of loyalty involved killing one of the rebels who had threatened his master. Citing his bravery, the Assembly rewarded July with "his Freedom and a Present of a Suit of Clothes."[82] Other slaves who had "behaved themselves well" received not liberty but clothes made with "blue Stroud, faced up with Red, and trimmed with brass Buttons."[83] In all, the Assembly rewarded over thirty slaves for their "great service in opposing the rebellious Negroes" in addition to a number of Indians who hunted and captured those rebels who escaped the final skirmish.[84]

These decisions by slaves raise questions about the degree to which lowcountry slaves had developed a sense of solidarity in the face of their collective oppression. The collusion between slave and slaveholder suggests that expressions of solidarity and community among slaves across the lowcountry was fairly fragile. That several slaves came to the aid of their embattled owners suggests that they identified with the interests of their master and household rather than with their potential liberators. Slaves like July may have been acting in a purely pragmatic way. Those who could have joined the rebellion may have weighed the chances of its possible success against the retribution that failure would bring. A large number of prospective rebels perhaps elected to cling to the few rights and privileges that they had extracted from their masters rather than join an endeavor that may have seemed foolhardy.

As the ranks of the rebels "increased every minute by New Negroes coming to them," some slaves clearly decided to take their chances with Jemmy.[85] Ambiguous about how many took this course of action, reports indicated that "they were above Sixty, some a hundred" as the afternoon drew on.[86] The slaves of St. Paul's would have learned of the uprising in several ways. The rebels obtained some drums and flags—perhaps from Hutchenson's store—by which they announced their presence to the farms and plantations of St. Paul's Parish, enabling them to get a number of slaves to rally to their "Colours displayed." Moreover, as they marched in this formation, their consciousness revealed itself, as they were reported "calling out Liberty."

This idea, so powerfully symbolized by St. Augustine, suggests that Jemmy and his followers may have understood the political character of their actions. Alternatively, it is possible that this incident of the rebellion was fabricated by an official who, wishing to vindicate the militia's violent response, imbued the insurgents' actions with an ideological design. By placing an emphasis on the revolt's political content, the Assembly would believe itself to be fully justified by their aggressive suppression of the rebellions, the rough justice administered to the rebels, and the draconian laws that they passed some months later.[87]

In addition to serving a practical purpose, the use of drums and banners were integral to methods of fighting in west-central Africa. It is worth repeating, moreover, that many African men who found themselves caught in the Atlantic trade were veterans of conflicts. Thus, it is entirely possible that some of the Stono rebels had prior military service and, as John Thornton has demonstrated, rebels' tactics bore some hallmarks of the style of fighting practiced by the armies of Kongo-Angola.[88] Just as Jemmy's followers beat drums to recruit other slaves to their cause, Kongo soldiers launched their attacks by striking "large kettle drums . . . with small clubs of ivory."[89] As ranks formed on the battlefield, other soldiers began "dancing and beating drums" to inspire the army as fighting commenced. By employing similar tactics, the rebels reproduced aspects of the martial culture of their former lives through the use of banners and drums. As they adopted this posture, these men became, as Vincent Harding has observed, "warriors again," perhaps resurrecting the masculine cast of military life that they had experienced in Africa.[90]

This moment was short-lived, however. Having "discerned the approaching Danger with time enough to avoid it," Bull alerted the militia, who, after posting pickets at strategic crossroads and ferry crossings, set out to find the rebels.[91] Hastily assembling themselves into a patrol, local farmers and planters joined the militia, and together they stumbled on the rebels near the Jacksonborough ferry on the Edisto River's eastern shore at about 4 P.M.[92] Believing that they were "victorious over the Whole Province" and intending "to draw more Negroes to them," the slaves had begun to dance, sing, and consume their plunder. Again, such behavior not only has its ethnic antecedents in Kongo military tradition, where victorious troops celebrated in similar ways, but it also gave the rebels further opportunity to undermine and invert the symbols of authority by engaging in actions deemed illegal by their masters. [. . .]

The transformation of the South Carolina lowcountry from a thinly populated frontier to a thickly inhabited plantation zone led to the degradation of slave work from a regime characterized by self-direction, semi-autonomy, and skill into one notable for its routine and discipline. The partial reconstruction of the agricultural practices of Atlantic Africa along the lowcountry's ranching and lumbering frontier possibly ameliorated enslavement for the first generation of slaves. The gradual but steady rise in work regimentation as rice cultivation began to dominate the economy and slave life perhaps fostered feelings of frustration as plantation agriculture supplanted pastoral farming. [. . .]

The fundamental negation of their masculinity and the transgression of their understanding of customary gender roles may have provided the circumstances that drove Jemmy and his followers onto a path of insurrection. As they crossed St. Paul's Parish, the rebels were able to reassert themselves as African men and to articulate a consciousness that was firmly rooted in their opposition to the social and cultural legacy of the rice revolution.

## Notes

1. For additional discussion see Margaret Washington Creel, *A Peculiar People: Slave Religion and Community-Culture among the Gullahs* (New York: New York University Press, 1988), pp. 33–34, 114–16; Robert M. Weir, *Colonial South Carolina: A History* (Millwood, N.Y.: KTO, 1983), pp. 193–94; Michael Mullin, *Africa in America: Slave Acculturation and Resistance in the American South and the British Caribbean, 1736–1831* (Urbana: University of Illinois Press, 1992), pp. 43–45. I wish to acknowledge Prof. Philip Curtin and members of the 1995 National Endowment for the Humanities Summer Seminar on Slavery and the New World Plantation Complex and the anonymous readers at *Slavery and Abolition* for their helpful comments and close readings of earlier drafts. I also wish to thank Profs. Kathleen Brown, Charles Cohen, and Leslie Schwalm for their advice, support, and encouragement.

2. Alexander Hewatt, *An Historical Account of the Rise and Progress of the Colonies of South Carolina and Georgia*, 2 vols. (London: Donaldson, 1779), rpt. in *Historical Collections of South Carolina*, ed. B. R. Carroll (New York: Harper, 1836), vol. 1, p. 333.

3. Peter H. Wood, *Black Majority: Negroes in Colonial South Carolina from 1670 through the Stono Rebellion* (New York: Knopf, 1974), pp. 308–26. For Darold D. Wax, Stono was "the most serious slave uprising in colonial America." See "'The Great Risque We Run': The Aftermath of Slave Rebellion at Stono, 1739–1745," *Journal of Negro History* 67 (Summer 1982): 136–47.

4. M. Eugene Sirmans, *Colonial South Carolina: A Political History, 1663–1763* (Chapel Hill: University of North Carolina Press, 1966), p. 208. Agreeing with Sirmans's assessment, Mullin writes that "Stono was not a climax." See Mullin, *Africa in America*, pp. 317–18, n. 33.

5. John K. Thornton, "African Dimensions of the Stono Rebellion," *American Historical Review* 96 (October 1991): 1113.

6. Joan Scott, "Gender: A Useful Category of Historical Analysis," in her *Gender and the Politics of History* (New York: Columbia University Press, 1988), pp. 28–50.

7. The term "rice revolution" is taken from Ira Berlin, "The Slave Trade and the Development of Afro-American Society in English Mainland North America, 1619–1775," *Southern Studies* 20 (Summer 1981): 129.

8. Russell R. Menard, "Financing the Lowcountry Export Boom: Capital and Growth in Early South Carolina," *William and Mary Quarterly* 3rd ser., 41 (October 1994): 659 [hereafter *WMQ*]; see also Peter A. Coclanis, *The Shadow of a Dream: Economic Life and Death in the South Carolina Low Country, 1670–1920* (New York: Oxford University Press, 1989), p. 64.

9. On population, see Wood, "The Changing Population of the Colonial South: An Overview of Race and Region, 1685–1790," in *Powhatan's Mantle: Indians in the Colonial Southeast*, ed.

Wood, Gregory A. Waselkov, and M. Thomas Hatley (Lincoln: University of Nebraska Press, 1989), p. 38; see also Coclanis, *Shadow of a Dream*, p. 64.

10. John S. Otto, "Livestock Raising in Early South Carolina, 1670–1700: Prelude to the Rice Plantation Economy," *Agricultural History* 61 (Fall 1987): 13–24; Wood, *Black Majority*, p. 31.

11. *Records of the Register and Secretary, 1675–1696*, cited in Aaron M. Shatzman, *Servants into Planters: The Origin of an American Image: Land Acquisition and Status Mobility in Seventeenth-Century South Carolina* (New York: Garland, 1989), p. 46. Wood also refers to this incident, although he calls the farmer Denys Omahone. See Wood, *Black Majority*, p. 31.

12. Shatzman, *Servants into Planters*, p. 113; John Lawson, *A New Voyage to Carolina*, ed.Hugh Talmage Lefler (Chapel Hill: University of North Carolina Press, 1967), p. 34.

13. Thomas Ashe, *Carolina; or A Description*, in *Historical Collections*, ed. Carroll, vol. 2, p. 73. As no tigers have ever lived in the Carolina lowcountry, Ashe presumably was referring to cougars.

14. James Glen, "Estimate of the Value of South Carolina," in *The Colonial South Carolina Scene: Contemporary Views, 1697–1774*, ed. H. Roy Merrens (Columbia: University of South Carolina Press, 1977), p. 186.

15. Samuel Wilson, "An Account of the Province of Carolina," in *Historical Collections*, ed. Carroll, vol. 2, p. 30; Ashe, *Carolina*, in ibid., vol. 2, pp. 72–73. See also "Letters from John Steward to William Dunlop," ed. Mabel L. Webber, *South Carolina Historical and Genealogical Magazine* 32 (January 1931): 22; on cattle-pen development, see Gary S. Dunbar, "Colonial Carolina Cowpens," *Agricultural History* 3 (July 1961): 125–31.

16. [John Norris], "Interview with James Freeman," in *Colonial South Carolina Scene*, ed. Merrens, p. 49.

17. For another perspective on pastoral agriculture, see Emmanuel Le Roy Ladurie's fascinating discussion on the life of the shepherd in the Pyrenees in *Montaillou: Cathars and Catholics in a French Village, 1294–1324*, trans. Barbara Bray (London: Scolar, 1980), pp. 103–35.

18. William DeBrahm, *Report of the General Survey in the Southern District of North America*, ed. Louis De Vorsey Jr. (Columbia: University of South Carolina Press, 1971), p. 95; *South Carolina and American General Gazette*, February 18, 1779. See also "A Gentleman's Account of His Travels, 1733–1734," in *Colonial South Carolina Scene*, ed. Merrens, p. 119. This particular traveler noted how planters "frequently settle their cow pens" on savannas, further observing that at least one pen stood six miles from the main plantation house.

19. These traditions of independent food production during slaves' free time may have played a critical role in the development of provision grounds and the task system that configured labor on rice plantations. See Philip D. Morgan, "Work and Culture: The Task System and the World of Lowcountry Blacks, 1700 to 1880," *WMQ* 3rd ser., 39 (October 1982): 563–99; Morgan, "Task and Gang Systems: The Organization of Labor on New World Plantations," in *Work and Labor in Early America*, ed. Stephen Innes (Chapel Hill: University of North Carolina Press, 1988), pp. 189–220.

20. [John Norris], *Profitable Advice for Rich and Poor in a Dialogue between James Freeman, a Carolina Planter, and Simon Question, a West Country Farmer* (London: Howe, 1712), p. 89.

21. Thornton, *The Kingdom of Kongo: Civil War and Transition, 1641–1718* (Madison: University of Wisconsin Press, 1983), p. 29.

22. Robert Norris, *Memoirs of the Reign of Bossa Ahadee, King of Dahomey* (London: Lowndes, 1798), p. 143. Norris later became an ardent abolitionist. See Robin Law, *The Slave Coast of West Africa, 1550–1750: The Impact of the Atlantic Slave Trade on an African Society* (Oxford: Clarendon Press / New York: Oxford University Press, 1991), pp. 1–2. For other observations about the role of women in the coastal regions of Atlantic Africa, see Henry Meredith, *An Account of the Gold Coast, with a Brief History of the African Company* (London: Longman, Hurst, Rees, Orme & Brown, 1812), p. 76; Thomas Winterbottom, *An Account of the Native Africans in the Neighbourhood of Sierra Leone*, 2 vols. (London: Whittingham, 1803), p. 145; Richard Jobson, *The Golden Trade, or a Discovery of the River Gambra and the Golden Trade of the Aethiopians* (London: Okes, 1623), p. 49. For modem discussions of this topic, see Claude Meillassoux, "Female Slavery," in *Women and Slavery in Africa*, ed. Claire C. Robertson and Martin A. Klein (Madison: University of Wisconsin Press, 1983), pp. 49–66; James F. Searing, *West African Slavery and Atlantic Commerce: The Senegal River Valley, 1700–1860* (New York: Cambridge University Press, 1993), pp. 120–23.

23. Jan Vansina, *Paths in the Rainforests: Toward a History of Political Tradition in Equatorial Africa* (Madison: University of Wisconsin Press, 1990), pp. 83–85.

24. Thornton, *Kingdom of Kongo*, p. 29. See also Walter Rodney, *A History of the Upper Guinea Coast, 1545 to 1800* (Oxford: Clarendon Press, 1970), pp. 18–19; Filippo Pigafetta, *A Report of the Kingdom of Congo and of the Surrounding Countries, Drawn Out from the Writings and Discourses of the Portuguese Duarte Lopez*, trans. and ed. Margarite Hutchinson (London: Cass, 1970), p. 19; Joseph C. Miller, *Way of Death: Merchant Capitalism and the Angolan Slave Trade, 1730–1830* (Madison: University of Wisconsin Press, 1988).

25. Meredith, *Account of the Gold Coast*, p. 76.

26. See Y. Person, "The Coastal Peoples: From Casamance to the Ivory Coast Lagoons," in *The General History of Africa*, vol. 4, *Africa from the Twelfth to the Sixteenth Century*, ed. D. T. Niane (London: Heinemann / Berkeley: University of California Press, 1984), pp. 310–23; Graham Connah, *African Civilizations: Precolonial Cities and States in Tropical Africa: An Archaeological Perspective* (Cambridge & New York: Cambridge University Press, 1987), pp. 97–120.

27. Jobson, *Golden Trade*, p. 49.

28. Andrew B. Smith, *Pastoralism in Africa: Origins and Development Ecology* (London: Hurst, 1992), pp. 72–98; John G. Galenty and Pierre Bonte, "Introduction," in *Herders, Warriors, and Traders: Pastoralism in Africa*, ed. Galenty and Bonte (Boulder: Westview, 1991), pp. 3–30.

29. Jean Barbot, *Barbot on Guinea: The Writings of Jean Barbot on West Africa, 1678–1712*, 2 vols., ed. P. E. H. Hair, Adam Jones, and Robin Law (London: Hakluyt Society, 1992), vol. 1, p. 103.

30. Barbot, *Barbot on Guinea*, vol. 1, p. 101; see also B. Barry, "Senegambia from the Sixteenth to the Eighteenth Century: Evolution of the Wolof, Sereer and 'Tukuloor,'" in *The General History of Africa*, vol. 5, *Africa from the Sixteenth to the Eighteenth Century*, ed. B. A. Ogot (London: Heinemann / Berkeley: University of California Press, 1992), pp. 262–99.

31. See Orlando Patterson, *Slavery and Social Death: A Comparative Study* (Cambridge, Mass.: Harvard University Press, 1982), p. 79.

32. The literature on Atlantic African ways in the lowcountry is fairly extensive; see, for example, Leland Ferguson, *Uncommon Ground: Archaeology and Early African America, 1650–1800* (Washington, D.C.: Smithsonian Institution Press, 1992); Creel, *A Peculiar People*; Joseph

Holloway, "The Origins of African-American Culture," in *Africanisms in American Culture*, ed. Holloway (Bloomington: Indiana University Press, 1990), pp. 1–18; Wood, *Black Majority;* Littlefield, *Rice and Slaves*. For more general discussions, see Robert Farris Thompson, *Flash of the Spirit: African and Afro-American Art and Philosophy* (New York: Vintage, 1984), pp. 101–60; Roger Bastide, *African Civilizations in the New World* (New York: Harper & Row, 1971); Sidney Mintz and Richard Price, *The Birth of African-American Culture: An Anthropological Perspective* (1976; reprint, Boston: Beacon, 1992).

33. On work and dignity, see Patrick Joyce, "The Historical Meaning of Work: An Introduction," in *The Historical Meaning of Work*, ed. Joyce (Cambridge and New York: Cambridge University Press, 1987), pp. 1–30.

34. The literature on the slave trade to South Carolina is substantial; see Littlefield, *Rice and Slaves;* Littlefield, "'Abundance of Negroes of That Nation': The Significance of African Ethnicity in Colonial South Carolina," in *The Meaning of South Carolina History: Essays in Honor of George C. Rogers, Jr.*, ed. David R. Chesnutt and Clyde N. Wilson (Columbia: University of South Carolina Press, 1991), pp. 19–38; Littlefield, "The Slave Trade to Colonial South Carolina: A Profile," *South Carolina Historical Magazine* 91 (April 1990): 68–99; W. Robert Higgins, "Charleston: Terminus and the Entrepot of the Colonial Slave Trade," in *The African Diaspora: Interpretive Essays*, ed. Martin L. Kilson and Robert I. Rotberg (Cambridge, Mass.: Harvard University Press, 1976); Higgins, "The Geographical Origins of Negro Slaves in Colonial South Carolina," *South Atlantic Quarterly* 70 (Winter 1971): 34–47; David Richardson, "The British Slave Trade to Colonial South Carolina," *Slavery and Abolition* 12 (December 1991): 125–72.

35. The information on slave imports into South Carolina is both incomplete and somewhat contradictory. Material on 1717 and 1718 slave imports drawn from Shipping Returns, CO5/508, PRO, and "The Record of Annual Slave Imports, 1706–1739," *Gentleman's Magazine* 25 (1755): 344, cited in Wood, *Black Majority*, p. 151. For further discussions on this topic, see previous note.

36. Menard, "The Africanization of the Lowcountry Labor Force," in *Race and Family in the Colonial South*, ed. Winthrop D. Jordan and Sheila L. Skemp (Jackson: University Press of Mississippi, 1987), pp. 81–108.

37. Littlefield, *Rice and Slaves;* see also Wood, "'It Was a Negro Taught Them': A New Look at African Labor in South Carolina," *Journal of Asian and African Studies* 9 (1974): 160–69; Judith A. Carney, "From Hands to Tutors: African Expertise in the South Carolina Rice Economy," *Agricultural History* 67 (Summer 1993): 1–30 [hereafter *AH*].

38. On the Loango trade, see Richardson, "Slave Exports from West Africa and West-Central Africa, 1700–1810: New Estimates of Volume and Distribution," *Journal of African History* 30 (1989): 19–20 [hereafter *JAH*]; Phyllis M. Martin, *The External Trade of the Loango Coast, 1576–1870: The Effects of the Changing Commercial Relations on the Vili Kingdom of Loango* (Oxford: Clarendon Press, 1972), pp. 73–92; Miller, *Way of Death*, pp. 549–51.

39. Entries of Negroes, September 29, 1738 to September 29, 1739, Records of the Public Treasurer, South Carolina Department of Archives and History; see also Shipping Returns, CO5/511, PRO. Thornton, however, has raised questions about the provenance of slaves labeled "Angolan," arguing that the Portuguese in Angola traded primarily with Brazilian rather than English merchants. These slaves came instead from the kingdom of Kongo, whose merchants traded with the English-based Royal African Company at Kabinda, near the mouth of the Zaire

River. See Thornton, "African Dimensions," p. 1104; K. G. Davies, *The Royal African Company* (New York: Atheneum, 1970), p. 231.

40. Richardson, "British Slave Trade to Colonial South Carolina," p. 133.

41. See David Geggus, "Sex Ratio, Age and Ethnicity in the Atlantic Slave Trade: Data from French Shipping and Plantation Records," *JAH* 30 (1989): 25. Although he looks primarily at the French trade, Geggus does draw some broad conclusions for the entire Atlantic commerce. With some qualification, these findings are generally supported by Paul Lovejoy, who notes, throughout the course of the Atlantic trade, "that 64.4% of the slaves were male and 35.6% were female." See Lovejoy, "The Impact of the Atlantic Slave Trade on Africa: A Review of the Literature," *JAH* 30 (1989): 381.

42. On charter groups, see T. H. Breen, "Creative Adaptations: Peoples and Cultures," in *Colonial British America: Essays in the New History of the Early Modern Era*, ed. Jack P. Greene and J. R. Pole (Baltimore: Johns Hopkins University Press, 1984), pp. 195–232.

43. Mintz and Price, *Birth of African-American Culture*, p. 50.

44. Vansina, *Kingdoms of the Savanna* (Madison: University of Wisconsin Press, 1966), pp. 60–61, 151–52; Anne Hilton, "European Sources for the Study of Religious Change in Sixteenth and Seventeenth Century Kongo," *Paideuma: Mitteilungen zur Kulturkunde* 33 (1987): 289–312; Thornton, "The Development of an African Catholic Church in the Kingdom of the Kongo, 1491–1750," *JAH* 25 (1984): 147–67.

45. Martin, *External Trade of the Loango Coast*, pp. 73–92; Davies, *Royal African Company*, pp. 231–32.

46. Lovejoy, "Impact of the Atlantic Slave Trade on Africa," p. 382; see also Geggus, "Sex Ratio, Age and Ethnicity," pp. 36–43.

47. See Lovejoy, *Transformations in Slavery: A History of Slavery in Africa* (Cambridge & New York: Cambridge University Press, 1983), pp. 68–96; Thornton, "African Soldiers in the Haitian Revolution," *Journal of Caribbean History* 25 (1993): 58–80; Thornton, "The Art of War in Angola, 1575–1680," *Comparative Studies in Society and History* 30 (April 1988): 360–78.

48. See Joyce E. Chaplin, *An Anxious Pursuit: Agricultural Innovation and Modernity in the Lower South, 1730–1815* (Chapel Hill: University of North Carolina Press, 1993), pp. 37–38, 227–76; Coclanis, *Shadow of a Dream*, pp. 48–110; John J. McCusker and Menard, *The Economy of British America, 1607–1789* (Chapel Hill: University of North Carolina Press, 1985), pp. 169–88.

49. *American Husbandry*, ed. Harry J. Carman (London, 1775; reprint, New York: Columbia University Press, 1939), p. 275. See also series Z, pp. 481–85, 486–92, and 493–99, in U.S. Bureau of the Census, *Historical Statistics of the United States: Colonial Times to 1970*, 2 vols. (Washington, D.C.: U.S. Department of Commerce, Bureau of Statistics, 1975), vol. 2, pp. 1192–93; James M. Clifton, "The Rice Trade in Colonial America," *AH* 55 (July 1981): 266–83; Henry C. Dethloff, "The Colonial Rice Trade," *AH* 56 (January 1982): 231–43; David O. Whitten, "American Rice Cultivation, 1680–1980: A Tercentary Critique," *Southern Studies* 21 (Spring 1982): 5–26.

50. Coclanis, *Shadow of a Dream*, p. 64.

51. Wood, *Black Majority*, pp. 35–62; Littlefield, *Rice and Slaves*; Carney, "From Hands to Tutors"; for an anthropological study of rice cultivation in southwestern Senegal, see Marc R. Schloss, *The Hatchet's Blood: Separation, Power and Gender in Ehing Social Life* (Tucson: University of Arizona Press, 1988).

52. On rice production in Atlantic Africa, see Littlefield, *Rice and Slaves,* pp. 74–114; see also Wood, "'It Was a Negro Taught Them.'"

53. Nicholas Owens, *Journal of a Slave-Dealer,* ed. Eveline Martin (London: Routledge, 1930), p. 52; see also George E. Brooks, *Landlords and Strangers: Ecology, Society, and Trade in Western Africa, 1000–1630* (Boulder: Westview, 1993), pp. 282–319; Carol MacCormack, "Wono: Institutionalized Dependence in Sherbro Descent Groups," in *Slavery in Africa: Historical and Anthropological Perspectives,* ed. Suzanne Miers and Igor Kopytoff (Madison: University of Wisconsin Press, 1977), pp. 181–204.

54. Capt. Samuel Gamble, *A Journal of a Voyage from London to Africa in the Sandown* (1793–1794), Log M121, National Maritime Museum, Greenwich, London; see also Littlefield, *Rice and Slaves,* pp. 93–95; Carney, "From Hands to Tutors," pp. 14–15.

55. Winterbottom, *Account of the Native Africans,* vol. 1, p. 145: see also John Matthews, *Voyage to the River Sierra-Leone* (London: White & Sewell, 1788), p. 56. In a 1620 account, there is some discussion of men working in the fields for a very limited time, helping with tillage and harvest; see Jobson, *Golden Trade,* p. 49. Most travelers' accounts, however, describe women as the primary field workers.

56. Pigafetta, *Report of the Kingdom of Congo,* p. 67; Miller, *Way of Death,* p. 417.

57. Thomas Nairne, *A Letter from South Carolina* (London: Baldwin, 1710), p. 59; "Johann Martin Bolzius Answers a Questionnaire on Carolina and Georgia," ed. Klaus G. Leowald et al., *WMQ* 3rd ser., 14 (April 1957): 258. On the role of slave women and men in rice production, see Thomas Porcher Plantation Diary, Stoney Porcher Papers, Southern Historical Collection, University of North Carolina, Chapel Hill; "Observations on the Culture of Rice," William Butler Papers, Southern Historical Collection; List of Negroes, Charles Cotesworth Pinckney Papers, Duke University.

58. See James C. Scott, *Weapons of the Weak: Everyday Forms of Peasant Resistance* (New Haven: Yale University Press, 1985), p. 43; Frances Fox Piven and Richard A. Cloward, *Poor People's Movements: Why They Succeed, How They Fail* (New York: Pantheon, 1977), p. 20.

59. Jan Rogozinski, *A Brief History of the Caribbean: From the Arawak and the Carib to the Present* (New York: Facts on File, 1992), p. 158.

60. See Wood, *Black Majority,* pp. 239–70; and Morgan, "Colonial South Carolina Runaways: Their Significance for Slave Culture," *Slavery and Abolition* 6 (December 1985): 57; see also Daniel Meaders, "South Carolina Fugitives as Viewed through Local Colonial Newspapers with Emphasis on Runaway Notices, 1732–1801," *Journal of Negro History* 60 (April 1975): 288–319. The data presented below was drawn from the *South Carolina Gazette* from February 1732 until September 1739. Using D-Base 3, I entered 253 cases, categorizing them by name, sex, date, age, place of birth, residence, owner, skin color, method of escape, number in escape, goods stolen, destination, skill, mode of transportation, and language abilities. See Edward A. Pearson, "From Stono to Vesey: Slavery, Resistance and Ideology in South Carolina" (Ph.D diss., University of Wisconsin, 1992), pp. 110–14.

61. Michael Johnson has noted that "the typical runaway was a young man who absconded alone"; see "Runaway Slaves and the Slave Communities in South Carolina, 1799 to 1830," *WMQ* 3rd ser., 38 (July 1981): 418. Meaders supports this conclusion, noting that "the average runaway was male, single, between the ages of eighteen and thirty"; see Meaders, "South Carolina Fugitives," p. 292.

62. On this topic, see Mullin, *Flight and Rebellion: Slave Resistance in Eighteenth-Century Virginia* (New York: Oxford University Press, 1972) .

63. In his study of slave resistance in eighteenth-century Virginia, Mullin argues that "acculturation—the changes by which African customs fell away as he acquired English and occupational specialization—ultimately created slaves who were able to challenge the security of the society itself." See *Flight and Rebellion*, p. 161.

64. Thornton has suggested that the rebels may have come from the Kongo, a kingdom that conducted its slave trade largely with the English-run Royal African Company, and not from Angola, whose traders sold slaves primarily to Portuguese merchants who shipped them directly to Brazil. The contemporary report that indicates the rebels to be "some Angola Negroes," titled "An Account of the Negroe Insurrection in South Carolina," identifies them, Thornton argues, incorrectly. See Thornton, "African Dimensions," p. 1103. On the relationship between the Angolan slave trade and Brazil, see Herbert S. Klein, *African Slavery in Latin America and the Caribbean* (New York: Oxford University Press, 1986), pp. 67–88; Kátia M. de Queirós Mattoso, *To Be a Slave in Brazil, 1550–1888* (New Brunswick, N.J.: Rutgers University Press, 1986), pp. 7–32; Miller, *Way of Death*.

65. *Virginia Gazette*, August 19–26, 1737; October 4, 1737, *The Journal of the Commons House of Assembly, 1736–1750*, ed. J. H. Easterby et al., vol. 1, *1736–1739* (Columbia: Historical Commission of South Carolina, 1951–1962), p. 330 [hereafter *JCHA*].

66. *South Carolina Gazette*, October 5, 1738, August 24, 1738, and September 25, 1738, in "The Journal of William Stephens," in *The Colonial Records of the State of Georgia*, vol. 4, *Stephens' Journal 1737–1740*, ed. Allen D. Candler (Atlanta: Franklin, 1906), pp. 190, 423; see also John Duffy, "Eighteenth-Century Health Conditions," *Journal of Southern History* 18 (August 1952): 289–302.

67. Walter J. Fraser Jr., *Charleston! Charleston! The History of a Southern City* (Columbia: University of South Carolina Press, 1989), pp. 64–65; Wood, *Black Majority*, p. 315.

68. Thomas Broughton to Lords Commissioners of Plantations, February 6, 1737, Original Correspondence, Secretary of State, CO5/388, PRO; see also *Pennsylvania Gazette*, March 10, 1737.

69. See Vincent Crapanzano, *Waiting: The Whites of South Africa* (New York: Random House, 1985), pp. 44–45; Ranajit Guha, *Elementary Aspects of Peasant Insurgency in Colonial India* (Delhi: Oxford University Press, 1983), p. 245.

70. "Governor William Bull's Representation of the Colony, 1770," in *Colonial South Carolina Scene*, ed. Merrens, p. 260.

71. Ibid.

72. A number of slaves who made this journey took various items with them, including blankets, tools, and clothes.

73. See Scott, *Domination and the Arts of Resistance: Hidden Transcripts* (New Haven: Yale University Press, 1990), pp. 166–82; for further discussions of practices of inversion in a European setting, see Natalie Zemon Davis, *Society and Culture in Early Modern France* (Stanford, Calif.: Stanford University Press, 1975), pp. 92–123; Ladurie, *Carnival in Romans: A People's Uprising at Romans, 1579–1580* (New York: Braziller, 1979).

74. *South Carolina Gazette*, April 6, 1734. On this practice, see Wood, *Black Majority*, pp. 283–84.

75. *South Carolina Gazette*, April 5, 1739.

76. Ibid., January 22, 1732.

77. Law, "'My Head Belongs to the King': On the Political and Ritual Significance of Decapitation in Pre-Colonial Dahomey," *JAH* 30 (1989): 399–415.

78. Law, *Slave Coast of West Africa*, pp. 97–98; Thomas Phillips, *A Journal of the Voyage Made in the Hannibal of London, Ann. 1693, 1694*, in *A Collection of Voyages and Travels*, 6 vols., trans. and ed. Awnsham Churchill and John Churchill (London: Walthoe, 1732), vol. 6, p. 220, cited in Law, *Slave Coast of West Africa*, p. 97.

79. "Account of the Negroe Insurrection in South Carolina" (undated, ca. 1740), in *Colonial Records of the State of Georgia*, ed. Allen D. Candler, Wm. J. Northern, and Lucian L. Knight (1904–1916; rept., New York: AMS, 1970), vol. 22, prt. 2, p. 232.

80. Ibid., p. 235.

81. November 29, 1739, *JCHA*, vol. 3, *1739–1741*, pp. 50–51, 64–65.

82. November 28, 1739, in ibid., p. 63.

83. November 28, 1739, in ibid., p. 65.

84. November 29, 1739, in ibid., pp. 64–65.

85. "Account of the Negroe Insurrection," p. 234.

86. Ibid.

87. On the aftermath of the rebellion, see Wax, "'The Great Risque We Run'"; Wood, *Black Majority*, pp. 320–26.

88. Thornton, "African Dimensions of the Stono Rebellion," pp. 1101–13; Thornton, "Art of War."

89. Pigafetta, *Report on the Kingdom of Congo*, p. 35

90. Vincent Harding, *There Is a River: The Black Struggle for Freedom in America* (New York: Harcourt Brace Jovanovich, 1981), p. 35.

91. Lt. Gov. William Bull to Board of Trade, October 5, 1739, CO5/367, PRO.

92. Hewatt, *Historical Account*, vol. 1, p. 332.

Essay 4

# TIME, RELIGION, REBELLION

## Mark M. Smith

We conclude with my own attempt to come to terms with the Stono Rebellion. Plainly, my understanding is indebted to previous interpretations, especially the ones advanced by Wood and Thornton. My concern is to establish why the slaves revolted when they did. My answer is found in the religious significance of the date of the rebellion and the icons used by the insurgents during the revolt. Although much of this essay agrees with the arguments offered by Wood and Thornton, the essay also departs from their work.

—•◦•—

On Sunday, September 9, 1739, sixty-odd South Carolina slaves took up arms and revolted, killing, as one terrified contemporary styled it, "twenty-three Whites after the most cruel and barbarous Manner."[1] [. . .] Why did the slaves revolt on the particular Sunday of September 9, 1739? The answer has implications beyond the immediate concern of chronology, for it highlights the importance of the rebels' memories of Catholicism generally and of the Kongolese veneration of the Virgin Mary specifically—memories that not only prove to have been crucial factors in the insurgents' timing and iconographic shaping of the rebellion, but that also have broader consequences for historians of eighteenth-century American slavery.

This article will carefully examine the timing of the Stono Rebellion in order to better reconceptualize and reevaluate our understanding of African acculturation in colonial North America. Stono's timing and religious geography expose the shortcomings of an older debate on the extent to which transplanted slaves retained elements of their "African" culture, and they also lend credence to recent work that examines the historically specific ways in which Africans who had already been exposed to Europeans prior to their forced relocation to the New World incorporated aspects of this culture into their own cosmologies. This more recent emphasis helps avoid an essentialist and temporally static notion of what is or is not

Source: Mark M. Smith, "Remembering Mary, Shaping Revolt: Reconsidering the Stono Rebellion," *Journal of Southern History* 67 (August 2001): 513–34. This edited version reprinted by permission of the managing editor of the *Journal of Southern History*.

"African" and instead allows for the possibility that pre-enslavement European-African contact might have helped shaped cultural systems and values in the context of New World slavery. [. . .][2]

[This essay is influenced by] the work of the Africanist John K. Thornton, who has explored the role of Afro-Catholicism and examined in detail the nature of Kongolese Catholicism prior to West Africans' transportation to South Carolina. Thornton builds on a fairly rich body of work dedicated to tracing Kongolese survivals in the Americas as well as on some earlier work on remnants of Kongolese Catholicism in the New World. For the most part, however, Afro-Protestantism has been the focus of most recent work, and historians have yet to develop in detail Thornton's analysis of Afro-Catholicism in shaping African American behavior in colonial America.[3] By examining the role of Kongolese Catholicism in shaping the form and deciding the timing of the Stono Rebellion in 1739, the argument advanced here will expand on Thornton's work in order to lend further meaning to his interpretation and will conclude with an assessment of how the analysis of Afro-Catholicism can help historians studying the cultural values, temporal consciousness, and modes of resistance of the enslaved in both colonial South Carolina and the Americas more generally.

Although we know a lot about the ethnic, religious, and strategic dynamics of the Stono Rebellion, the slaves' motivations for revolting when they did remain as inscrutable now as they were to the colony's white population then. The main reason for our frustratingly opaque understanding of the rebellion is obvious: The story of the revolt has been reconstructed mainly from elite, white sources. The slaves themselves (or, rather, the records) are silent on why they revolted when they did. Little wonder that one recent observer has concluded that the slaves' "precise motives and reasoning lie beyond historical inquiry."[4]

Given the dearth of slave testimony on the insurrection, historians who have examined the Stono incident have had to rely on hard logic, historical reasoning, and a good deal of speculation in an effort to uncover the slaves' motivations. Thornton's seminal 1991 reinterpretation of the Stono Rebellion is a case in point. He shows that "we can see the rebellion from a new angle if we consider the African contribution as well as the American one." His evidence is compelling, and his argument powerful. Slaves involved in the revolt—particularly the leaders—were not from Angola, as most earlier interpretations had it, but from the heavily Catholic Kongo, which for many years had been under the influence of Portuguese and Italian clerics. Moreover, "the Kongolese were proud of their Christian and Catholic heritage." Thornton demonstrates how this Catholic-Kongolese background manifested itself during the Stono Rebellion. Kongolese slaves in South Carolina responded to Spanish offers of freedom should they escape to St. Augustine. Thornton makes clear that these Portuguese-speaking slaves were literate and understood some Spanish. He also suggests that several of the rebellion's leaders may have been Kongolese soldiers. During the insurrection, they demonstrated their facility with guns (a skill developed in Kongo), Kongolese military tactics, and their martial use of banners or flags and drums. They danced and drilled like Kongolese warriors, fought like them, and struck out for religious as much as for political freedom. Most recent historians have tended to accept Thornton's general point that the Stono rebels were Kongolese Catholics.[5]

But does Thornton's emphasis explain the slaves' motivations and actions as fully as it might? On one important matter—the timing of the Stono Rebellion—Thornton accepts the prevailing wisdom advanced by Peter Wood that "the actual rebellion broke out on Sunday (normally a slave's day off), September 9, 1739," but neither Thornton nor Wood offer wholly convincing explanations for why slaves rebelled on this Sunday in particular. Thornton's silence is ironic, for the explanation of the revolt's timing may be found by scrutinizing both the slaves' Catholicism and their unwitting temporal adaptation to their Protestant environment in the New World. In short, the interpretation advanced here builds on both Wood's and Thornton's pioneering works in an effort to uncover the slaves' precise motivations for insurrection on the particular weekend of September 8–9. It suggests that they revolted when they did because of their specific veneration of the Virgin Mary, their general commitment to and understanding of the Catholic calendar developed in the Kongo, and because their temporal understanding of that calendar had necessarily undergone a silent (but ultimately incidental) transformation in their forced relocation to a predominantly Protestant plantation society. [. . .][6]

Wood, the only historian to have considered the timing of the Stono Rebellion in any detail, believes that July 1739 was an important month for creating an atmosphere of suspense and anticipation propitious for revolt. July, after all, saw a suspicious visit to several of South Carolina's coastal towns by a Spanish captain, a priest, and "a Negro . . . who spoke excellent English." Contemporaries agreed that such activity was suspect, and after the revolt they considered the priest in particular to have been "employed by the Spaniards to procure a general Insurrection of the Negroes." Also important, maintains Wood, was the yellow fever epidemic that swept through Charlestown in August and September, which proved sufficiently virulent to close the *South Carolina Gazette* and some schools for several weeks. Lieutenant Governor William Bull prorogued the Assembly because of the epidemic, and about six people a day perished during the late summer of 1739. "The confusion created by this sickness," argues Wood, ". . . may have been a factor in the timing of the Stono Rebellion." Indeed. With so many whites sick, revolt was plainly easier and stood a greater chance of success. But Wood sees two other factors as important influences in the timing of the revolt. First, slaves' calculations "might also have been influenced by the newspaper publication, in mid-August, of the Security Act which required all white men to carry firearms to church on Sunday or submit to a stiff fine, beginning on September 29. It had long been recognized that the free hours at the end of the week afforded the slaves their best opportunity for cabals. . . . " A literate slave involved in the rebellion, according to this reasoning, read of the Act on or shortly after August 18, 1739 (presumably in the *Gazette*), and realized that revolt had a better chance if it were to take place before Saturday, September 29. "Since the Stono Uprising, which caught planters at church, occurred only weeks before the published statute of 1739 went into effect," concludes Wood, "slaves may have considered that within the near future their masters would be even more heavily armed on Sundays." Second, he writes that "one other factor seems to be more than coincidental to the timing of the insurrection. Official word of hostilities between England and Spain . . . appears to have reached Charlestown the very weekend that the uprising began." This news, argues Wood, probably constituted "a logical trigger for rebellion."[7] It seems very likely that slaves knew illness had debilitated the white population; it is also clear that the Spanish had infiltrated the colony and promised freedom to slaves who escaped to St. Augustine. Although Wood shows that news of the hostilities between England and Spain did not reach Georgia until September 13 "with Letters of the 10th [a day after the revolt], from the Government at Charles-town," it is possible that rumors of war were heard earlier.[8] Certainly, Wood is right to suggest that slaves probably decided to revolt on a Sunday or weekend between August 18 and September 29: Churchgoing whites were distracted, and slaves had a little more room for maneuver on Sundays. Slaves also wanted to revolt before the provisions of the Security Act came into effect. But while most of this reasoning helps explain why the Stono Rebellion happened on a Sunday during the late summer of 1739, it cannot explain why it happened on Sunday, September 9, in particular. Between August 18, when news of the Security Act was published, and Saturday, September 29, when the act was to go into effect, there were six Sundays on which the slaves could have revolted (August 19 and 26; September 2, 9, 16, and 23). Most of the conditions sufficient for revolt—the epidemic among whites, rumors of war, Spanish offers of freedom—were still in place during these Sundays. Granting that rumors of war between England and Spain could have circulated in the week leading up to the Stono Rebellion, it is still reasonable to ask whether there were reasons in addition to those offered by Wood that help to explain why slaves revolted on the particular weekend of September 8–9 and not on the following two weekends instead.

The interpretation advanced here does not so much refute Wood but rather expands on the context-specific and immensely helpful framework he established nearly a quarter-century ago. In fact, the argument not only helps pinpoint the timing of the rebellion within Wood's broad temporal parameters but also builds on his discussion of the resonance of Africanisms throughout colonial South Carolina. The Stono Rebellion itself may be added to Wood's list of African influences because a syncretic version of Portuguese-Kongolese Catholicism played an important role in the timing and iconology of the rebellion. Even during a bloody insurrection, Kongolese-Catholic theological values found room for expression and helped empower its participants.

Thornton has produced a wealth of evidence to suggest that "the Kongolese of the eighteenth century regarded their Christianity as a fundamental part of their national identity. . . . " He suggests that Kongolese slaves in South Carolina, including those involved in the Stono insurgency, retained their commitment to Catholicism, and contemporary observers agreed.[9]

The Kongolese knew their Catholic calendar. For example, "the community would assemble on Saturdays and say the rosary, their principal regular religious observation." The educated elite led such meetings. But everyone, according to Thornton, observed the regular holidays. In addition to Easter and Advent-Christmas-Epiphany, "the biggest and most important holidays were Halloween–All Saints' Day and the day dedicated to Saint James Major, 25 July." Kongolese customs were at work here, thus reflecting a degree of cultural and religious syncretism: "Halloween and All Saints' Day provided Kongolese with a good opportunity to pay appropriate respect to their ancestors in a Christian tradition." On the whole, then, Kongolese were good Catholics. They were also punctual, albeit on their own terms.[10] Anne Hilton has explained that "they kept Lent fifteen days before Europe because they regulated it according to the moon. They kept the normal forty days." For nonmovable feasts, "the Capuchins gave them calendars so that they could warn the people of vigils and feasts." Plainly, these were calendar-conscious people. Whatever the degree of syncretism involved, though, one thing remains clear; Kongolese adhered to a Catholic calendar spotted with precise, important affective days and dates. They knew these dates and apparently remembered them. [. . .][11]

Although Hilton and Thornton differ on the extent to which Kongolese Christianity was syncretic, they agree on the importance of the Virgin Mary to the society's Catholicism. Beyond the Kongolese commitment to Catholicism generally, evidence suggests that the Virgin Mary occupied an important place in their cosmology. One woman had a vision in 1703 in which the Virgin advised her to tell her people to say the Hail Mary three times to avoid Christ's wrath, and thousands apparently took her counsel. Shortly thereafter another woman, Apollonia Mafuta, had a similar vision from the Virgin, the first of several.[12]

The observations of a Capuchin missionary, Father Jerom Merolla da Sorrento, who visited the Kongo in 1682, also confirm the celebrity of Mary in Kongolese cosmology. Upon his arrival in the region he noticed, for example, a church built by the Portuguese "and dedicated to the Virgin *Mary,* whose Statue [or] *Bassorelievo* [bas-relief], is constantly worship'd every Sunday by a vast number of *Negroes* who flock hither for that purpose." The priest encouraged the Kongolese veneration of Mary by advising parents to "enjoyn their Children to observe particular Devotion, such as to repeat so many times aday the *Rosary* or the *Crown* in honour of the blessed Virgin [and] to fast on Saturdays." The punctual observance of such affective times—common to both Catholicism and religious times generally—became a characteristic of Kongolese Christianity, for, in addition to the celebration of Saint James's Day, Sorrento noted that there were "other sorts of Feasts which are wont to be kept by the Blacks, such as upon the Birth-days of their Patrons."[13]

The advent of the Antonian movement associated with Dona Beatriz Kimpa Vita (ca. 1684–1706) in 1704 had the effect of relegating Mary to the status of a secondary saint. Sufficiently confident in her knowledge of Catholic doctrine, this young Kongolese woman set about critiquing colonial Portuguese rule. She reconfigured basic Catholic tenets by offering theological arguments based on those beliefs that used the religion of her oppressors to lead a movement dedicated to restoring the kingdom of Kongo. But even Dona Beatriz, who championed the supremacy of Saint Anthony, included the Virgin in her sermons against the established Catholic Church. In her desire to purify what she perceived as venal and racially biased Catholicism, Dona Beatriz argued for the existence of black saints; she also maintained, according to Thornton, that "Jesus and Mary were actually Kongolese" and that "Mary's mother was a slave of the Marquis Nzimba Mpangi when Mary gave Jesus birth." She went further, not only changing the words of the catechismal prayers but, most importantly, altering the Ave Maria and the Salve Regina, prayers addressed to the Virgin Mary. The revised prayer is worth quoting, for it is suggestive of the revolutionary and emancipatory power the Kongolese attached to Mary:

> Salve [Save] the Queen, mother of mercy, sweetness of life, our hope. *Deus* [God] save you; we cry out for you, we the exiled children of Eve; we sigh for you, kneeling and weeping in this valley of tears. Therefore, you, our advocate, cast your merciful eyes on us and after that exile show us Jesus, the fruit of your womb; Ehe, you the merciful, Ehe benevolent one! E sweet one! the perpetual Virgin Mary. Pray for us, Santa [Holy] Mother of Nzambi a Mpungu, so that we may be worthy of the promises of Christ.[14]

As Thornton explains, the final portion of the new prayer, while "reasserting the concept of advocacy of the Virgin," also "takes the virtues of Mary from the Salve Regina and substitutes Saint Anthony." The reasoning for this substitution need not concern us. Suffice it to note that, although Dona Beatriz's reformulation of the prayer placed Anthony above Mary, the Virgin still remained a powerful and protecting figure in Kongolese theology. With Dona Beatriz's burning at the stake in 1706, the Antonian movement lost momentum, and Kongolese veneration for the Virgin Mary—already very high anyway—only increased.[15]

The Virgin Mary, then, occupied a central role in Kongolese theology. Her statue was as commonplace as her picture. Mary's semblance was believed to have come from the sky and to carry the "protective functions of an *nkisi*—fetish—of the *nkadi* mpemba and sky spirit type." People from surrounding districts visited churches that housed statues of the Virgin, especially during times of calamity. Even Hilton, who stresses the highly syncretic nature of Kongolese Catholicism, sees Mary as particularly important to seventeenth- and eighteenth-century Kongolese Christianity: The Mwissikongo (the Kongolese elite), she writes, may well have "regarded the Virgin Mary as Christ's female co-chief."[16]

Her centrality to Kongolese spirituality was reflected in Mary's heightened iconological and theological status. The *mani Kongo*, the spiritual leader of the Mwissikongo and the intermediary between the living and the dead, led Mass on Holy Saturdays, when he displayed the most important of the royal insignia, the drum. "Moreover," remarks Hilton, "the Madonna was also associated with Saturday, which the Mwissikongo . . . took as the day of prayer and rest devoted especially to the dead."[17] There were other symbolic resonances associated with Mary. Thornton notes that "white was the color of the dead and of ancestors to the Kongolese," and the Virgin Mary was, in fact, a Kongolese ancestor, according to Dona Beatriz. But the color white—associated with the Virgin Mary—had further particular provenance in Kongolese history. Dom Afonso's fifteenth-century victory over the pagan Pango, for example, was, according to Filippo Pigafetta's 1591 rendition of Duarte Lopez's account, thanks to the appearance of a woman in white—very likely the Virgin Mary. They "owed their victory to the presence of a lady in white, whose dazzling splendour blinded the enemy." Memories of the event lingered. "By the eighteenth century," remarks Thornton, "Kongolese looked back [to] . . . Afonso I as the founder of the faith in Kongo." Churches in Kongo were accordingly dedicated to the Virgin, and representations of her were apparent throughout the region. In this way, the Virgin Mary seeped into Kongolese historical memory, religious discourse, and spiritual ritual. Plainly, the Virgin Mary had military and religious significance. Her appearance in white had dazzled the non-Christian enemy, and, in this sense, she emerged as savior and holy warrior, protector and advocate. [. . .][18]

Helpful though Thornton's pioneering work is, its heavy emphasis on militarism and on a broadly conceived Kongolese Catholicism blinds us to the specificity of slaves' actions and motivations during Stono. His general points on the manifestations of Kongolese Catholicism and martiality during the rebellion, particularly his emphasis on the rebels' use of drums, identifies some of the broad symbolic features of the insurrection, but his arguments lack precision. Was the behavior of Stono's rebels primarily and singularly militaristic? Is it possible to go beyond the identification of the revolt with Kongolese Catholicism generally by identifying specific Catholic traits apparent in the timing and features of the revolt? Moreover, in his zeal to establish the authenticity of the insurgents' Kongolese Christianity, Thornton sometimes slights the extent to which their Catholicism was necessarily altered in the New World. By focusing on their specific veneration of Mary, we can add detail to Thornton's notion of Kongolese Catholicism, thereby helping to better explain the actual timing and iconological landscape of the Stono Rebellion.

To take timing first: Most accounts place the beginning of the rebellion in the early hours of Sunday, September 9. In his recent examination of slavery in colonial South Carolina, Robert Olwell sensibly dates the preparations for the revolt—and, hence, its beginnings proper—as Saturday, September 8. He notes the publication of an advertisement in the *South Carolina Gazette* on that Saturday and remarks that "on the very night that this advertisement appeared, a group of slaves were secretly gathering on the banks of the Stono."[19] Although the Stono Rebellion broke out on Sunday, September 9, it was preceded by contemplation, planning, and preparatory gathering late on Saturday, September 8. The date is significant since, as previously noted, Saturdays in the Kongo were dedicated to Mary, and the *mani Kongo* led Mass using the royal insignia, the drum. Hilton notes that "the Madonna was also associated with Saturdays . . . the day of prayer and rest," and possibly also, in the context of enslavement, prayer and preparation. More importantly still, that specific Saturday, September 8, 1739, was the day of Nativity of the Virgin Mary, as even contemporary Protestant almanacs noted.[20] Given that, as Jerom Merolla da Sorrento remarked in 1682, the Kongolese usually feasted on certain days of observance "such as upon the Birth-days of their Patrons," it is possible that, of the weekends when South Carolina's Catholic slaves could have revolted, they chose the weekend of September 8–9 because it coincided with the nativity of an important, protecting, and empowering Kongolese religious icon.[21] Since no direct evidence exists to show that the Kongolese celebrated Mary's nativity specifically, the interpretation advanced here remains conjectural, although no more than that offered by Thornton concerning the martial symbols used in the rebellion. On the other hand, it seems likely that such a calendar-conscious Catholic people were quite aware of the auspicious date on which they revolted.[22]

If Stono's slaves did rebel with Mary in mind, a case needs to be made that they not only had the wherewithal and opportunity to ascertain the date, but also that they infused the revolt itself with Marian memories and images. Regarding the former, it is probable that the rebellion's slave leader(s) was aware of the date in the English colony. Most sources agree on the literacy of the rebellion's leader—whatever his name. George Cato recalled that "Cato was teached how to read and write by his rich master." Indeed, "long befo' dis uprisin', de Cato slave wrote passes for slaves and do all he can to send them to freedom." Other sources and virtually all historians agree on the literacy of the leader(s); Wood, for example, argues that slaves revolted on the heels of the publication of the Security Act in mid-August 1739—a consciousness of which implies the literacy of at least some of them. Stono's rebels were, therefore, probably capable of ascertaining the date, presumably from snatched glances at newspapers.[23]

Of the images and icons recruited by Stono's rebels, nineteenth-century accounts of the eighteenth-century incident are suggestive. One new piece of evidence offers important clues—a rather romantic, but surprisingly accurate, literary account of the rebellion published in the antislavery newspaper *Liberty Bell* in 1847. Although the names of the various participants seem invented (in place of Jemey/Jemmy or Cato is "Arnold"), [. . .] essential details can be corroborated. The account notes, for example, that Arnold was literate. The description of the unfolding of the revolt also rings true, although the numbers of "four or five hundred strong" are certainly exaggerated: "The day approached. It arrived. It was a Sunday. . . . Arnold repaired early to the slave-quarter and harangued the slaves upon a case of surpassing cruelty they had witnessed the night before. A tumult of excitement was gathered around him. The alarm spread." From the plantation, they headed "towards Stono, a small settlement about five miles off, where there was a warehouse full of arms and ammunition." As Wood put it, "the group proceeded to Stono Bridge and broke into Hutchenson's store, where small arms and powder were on sale." At the store, continues the 1847 account, the rebels armed themselves with guns, clubs, and axes. Revealingly, "a quantity of white cloth furnished them with banners. Drums and fifes were also in the warehouse. . . . So they took up their march towards Jacksonburgh, with drums beating and banners flying, in some show of military order." The account then details correctly the slaves' encounter with Lieutenant Governor Bull, the ensuing fight, and the quelling of the insurrection. The source seems reliable not least because it echoes some key details offered in other descriptions of the revolt.[24]

Although historians have focused on the iconography of the revolt by identifying the rebels' masculinity and their militaristic use of flags, dances, and drums, no one has considered the rebels' use of drums and white cloth in the context of their close identification with Mary and her central place in Kongolese Catholicism.[25] The cloth and its color, however, require attention. Thornton, who ignores the banner's color, unnecessarily dismisses Wood's suggestion that it may have had religious significance. Thornton argues that the banner was really a flag and typical of Kongolese military practice.[26] Recall, though, that the color white was associated closely with Mary in Kongolese iconography. In fact, it had both spiritual and martial significance: Was not Dom Afonso's fifteenth-century victory over Pango thanks to the appearance "of a lady in white whose dazzling splendour blinded the enemy"? Did not the Kongolese capital have a "Cathedral dedicated to *Our Lady of Victory*" that was "made of Mud, but whitened both within and without"? According to Thornton, "As Christians, Kongolese saw Europeans represented as Jesus, the saints, and the Virgin Mary in religious terms." In Dona Beatriz's visions and dreams, Europeans appeared as white not because of their skin color but because of their supposed affinity with the spiritual world.[27] Jesus, the saints, and Mary, then, were white because of their otherworldliness, and in the context of a rebellion against enslavers who preached an alien religion, the Stono rebels invoked the whiteness of one of the most powerful of Kongolese saints. By arming themselves with white cloth on the day after the Virgin's nativity, the insurgents invoked broad memories of Mary and specific recollections of Dom Afonso's famous victory over non-Christians. Cato, after all, even after the insurrection, supposedly proclaimed, "we 'is not converted.'"[28]

So too with the drums. Drums beaten by the slaves and the dancing that accompanied them have an exclusively martial meaning for Thornton and other historians; they were simply Kongolese military practices of no additional significance.[29] The royal drum was also associated with Holy Saturdays in the Kongo, the day of the Madonna. More generally, the Kongolese "beat their Drums with open hands" following Mass and catechism. Invoking the Virgin in this way held both religious and military significance to Stono's slaves. The two traditions and memories were not mutually exclusive; they were linked inextricably and braided tightly. Furthermore, because Mary and her images were mustered in a context in which enslaved people were striking out for freedom, Mary's significance became political. Indeed, the rebels shouted "Liberty," which, as Thornton shows, was "a word that, to those Kongolese who still thought in Kikongo as they spoke in English, was *lukangu*, whose root, *kanga*, also meant 'salvation' to a Christian." Stono's rebels summoned Mary temporally and iconologically—the two, in fact, were one and the same—because of her Kongolese historical significance and her protective and revolutionary power. This was neither the first nor the last time that Mary's iconographic power would be appropriated by the oppressed.[30] Stono's slaves saw, for all the reasons mentioned by Wood, that the general conditions for rebellion were ripe, but their memories of Mary helped shape the features, meaning, and precise timing of the revolt.

Conditions of bondage and the process of their enslavement nevertheless shaped the Stono slaves' Catholicism. For, plainly, although they prepared their revolt on September 8, it was Mary's nativity by the Protestant, Julian calendar—the predominant one in English-speaking South Carolina—not by the Gregorian, Catholic calendar, the use of which the English did not mandate until 1752. In fact, September 8–9, Julian style, was September 19–20, Gregorian style. In a bitter irony, then, Stono's slaves revolted, strictly speaking, on the "wrong" date. This is not surprising. How would they have known that they were revolting eleven days "early"? Perhaps they could have received such specific information from their Spanish informants, but it is quite unlikely that they could have maintained their temporal alignment with the Catholic calendar when the majority of whites around them used the Protestant one. Indeed, highly literate and informed Gregorian-style European travelers to the Julian-calendar American colonies sometimes had trouble remembering new-style dates, even though they had ready access to calendars and almanacs.[31] Probably the rebels had to rely on guarded glimpses at newspapers. In effect, then, the revolt is a good illustration of religious syncretism and the disruptive effects of slavery. Stono's rebels kept their liturgical calendar intact mentally, but the realities of slave labor and sometimes deliberate misinformation by slaveholders meant that they unwittingly acted as Afro-Catholics according to a non-Catholic calendar.[32] It hardly matters that the Stono rebels revolted on the "wrong" day. For them it was the "right" date and still held affective importance. Indeed, the insurgents' timing of their revolt illustrates with exquisite precision what some theorists of time have maintained—that time in all its guises is essentially an invented and subjective phenomenon. Calendrical time in this instance was constructed and not reducible to an ostensibly "true" date.[33]

To deny the possibility (or even probability) that the slaves who orchestrated the Stono revolt did so with the date of Mary's nativity in mind means to dismiss the images associated with Mary that the insurgents employed during the rebellion. Non-elite peoples in colonial North America did not lack a sense of time and of temporal rhythms and orders, particularly quite precise ones. Native Americans, for example, sometimes launched highly successful raids on particular dates because they understood the strategic and tactical advantages such dates afforded. During the Pontiac Wars, for example, they attacked Fort Michilimackinac on June 4, 1763 (the king's birthday), "which the Indians knew was a day set apart by the English as one of amusement and celebration," and managed to capture the fort as a result.[34] Calendrical consciousness, then, was not the exclusive provenance of the elite. Indeed, if Ira Berlin's recent argument concerning the sophisticated characteristics of Atlantic creole slaves is correct, Stono's leaders epitomized such qualities.[35] Memories of Kongolese history and Catholicism helped Stono's slaves prepare and rebel on days that were both strategically practical as well as spiritually empowering and propitious. [. . .]

## Notes

1. "Report of the Committee Appointed to Enquire into the Causes of the Disappointment of Success in the Late Expedition Against St. Augustine," July 1, 1741, in *The Colonial Records of South Carolina: The Journal of the Commons House of Assembly, May 18, 1741–July 10, 1742*, ed. J. H. Easterby et al. (Columbia: Historical Commission of South Carolina, 1953), pp. 78–93 (quotation on p. 83). [. . .] For their comments and suggestions on earlier versions of this article, I thank Ronald R. Atkinson, John Basil, Walter B. Edgar, Eugene D. Genovese, Daniel C. Littlefield, Philip D. Morgan, Robert Olwell, and the anonymous readers for the *Journal of Southern History*.

2. Melville J. Herskovits, *The Myth of the Negro Past* (New York & London: Harper, 1941); E. Franklin Frazier, *The Negro Church in America* (New York: Schocken, 1963). Their debate is usefully summarized in Joseph E. Holloway, "Introduction," in *Africanisms in American Culture*, ed. Holloway (Bloomington: Indiana University Press, 1990), pp. ix–xxi. For a critique of the timeless character often attached to African religions and the need to remain sensitive to

the evolution of African cosmologies over time and place, see *Themes in the Christian History of Central Africa*, ed. T. O. Ranger and John Weller (Berkeley: University of California Press, 1975), pp. 5–8; and the helpful discussion offered in Sylvia R. Frey and Betty Wood, *Come Shouting to Zion: African American Protestantism in the American South and British Caribbean to 1830* (Chapel Hill and London: University of North Carolina Press, 1998), pp. 1–3, and esp. pp. 35–62.

3. John K. Thornton, "African Dimensions of the Stono Rebellion," *American Historical Review* 96 (October 1991): 1101–13. On Kongolese legacies, see Robert Farris Thompson and Joseph Cornet, *The Four Moments of the Sun: Kongo Art in Two Worlds* (Washington, D.C.: National Gallery of Art, 1981); Thompson, *Flash of the Spirit: African and Afro-American Art and Philosophy* (New York: Random House, 1983); Thompson, "Kongo Influences on African-American Artistic Culture," in *Africanisms in American Culture*, ed. Holloway, pp. 148–84; Dena J. Epstein, *Sinful Tunes and Spirituals: Black Folk Music to the Civil War* (Urbana: University of Illinois Press, 1977), esp. pp. 95–96; and Roger Bastide, *The African Religions of Brazil: Toward a Sociology of the Interpenetration of Civilizations*, trans. Helen Sebba (Baltimore: Johns Hopkins University Press, 1978), esp. p. 347. See also John F. Szwed and Roger D. Abrahams, *Afro-American Folk Culture: An Annotated Bibliography of Materials from North, Central, and South America and the West Indies* (Philadelphia: Institute for the Study of Human Issues, 1978). For work on Afro-Protestantism that offers a few remarks on the Catholic backgrounds of some enslaved Africans, see Frey and Wood, *Come Shouting to Zion*, pp. 15–20. For recent thoughts on revolutionary Afro-Christian theology in shaping Denmark Vesey's plot, see Douglas R. Egerton, "'Why They Did Not Preach Up This Thing': Denmark Vesey and Revolutionary Theology," *South Carolina Historical Magazine* 100 (October 1999): 298–318. For a work that recognizes the importance of Catholicism to the slaves' cosmology in the colonial South, see Albert J. Raboteau, *Slave Religion: The "Invisible Institution" in the Antebellum South* (New York: Oxford University Press, 1978), pp. 87–89, 111–14, 271–75.

4. The main primary sources, which say little about the matter of motivation, are noted in Olwell, *Masters, Slaves, and Subjects: The Culture of Power in the South Carolina Low Country, 1740–1790* (Ithaca, N.Y.: Cornell University Press, 1998), p. 21 (quotation), and n. 8.

5. Thornton, "African Dimensions," pp. 1113 (first quotation), 1103 (second quotation). On the acceptance of Thornton's basic argument, see Morgan, *Slave Counterpoint: Black Culture in the Eighteenth-Century Chesapeake and Lowcountry* (Chapel Hill: University of North Carolina Press, 1998), pp. 386, 455–56; Ira Berlin, *Many Thousands Gone: The First Two Centuries of Slavery in North America* (Cambridge, Mass.: Belknap Press of Harvard University Press, 1998), pp. 72–73; Olwell, *Masters, Slaves, and Subjects*, pp. 21–25; Jane Landers, *Black Society in Spanish Florida* (Urbana: University of Illinois Press, 1999), p. 34. See also Landers, "Gracia Real de Santa Teresa de Mose: A Free Black Town in Spanish Colonial Florida," *American Historical Review* 95 (February 1990): 9–30, esp. 27.

6. Thornton, "African Dimensions," p. 1102 (quotation). For Wood's discussion of Stono's timing, see *Black Majority*, pp. 308–15.

7. Wood, *Black Majority*, pp. 312–14 (all quotations).

8. "The Journal of William Stephens," in *The Colonial Records of the State of Georgia*, vol. 4, *Stephens' Journal 1737–1740*, ed. Allen D. Candler (Atlanta: Franklin, 1906), p. 412 (also cited in Wood, *Black Majority*, p. 314, n. 25). The Charleston *South Carolina Gazette* for September 8, 1739, carried news, via Boston, of the outfitting of English privateers to attack Spanish merchant

ships, which, while not a declaration of war per se, could have helped spread the rumor that war was imminent.

9. Thornton, "African Dimensions," 1106–7 (quotations). For a corroborative contemporary account of the rebels' Catholicism, see "Extract of a Letter from S. Carolina, dated October 2," *Gentleman's Magazine* 10 (March 1740): 127–29. See also Landers, *Black Society*, p. 34; and Raboteau, *Slave Religion*, pp. 111–12.

10. Thornton, *The Kongolese Saint Anthony: Dona Beatriz Kimpa Vita and the Antonian Movement, 1684–1706* (Cambridge and New York: Cambridge University Press, 1998), pp. 27–35 (quotations on pp. 30 and 31). On the cultural subjectivism of definitions of punctuality, see Clifford Geertz, "Person, Time, and Conduct in Bali," in his *The Interpretation of Cultures: Selected Essays* (New York: Basic Books, 1973), pp. 360–411, esp. pp. 391–98; and Douglas Raybeck, "The Coconut-Shell Clock: Time and Cultural Identity," *Time and Society* 1 (September 1992): 323–40.

11. Anne Hilton, *The Kingdom of Kongo* (Oxford: Clarendon Press / New York: Oxford University Press, 1985), pp. 203 (first quotation), 205 (second quotation).

12. Thornton, *Kongolese Saint Anthony*, pp. 105, 108, 157. See also Georges Balandier, *Daily Life in the Kingdom of Kongo from the Sixteenth to the Eighteenth Century*, trans. Helen Weaver (London: Allen & Unwin, 1968), pp. 256–57.

13. Jerom Merolla da Sorrento, *A Voyage to Congo, and Several Other Countries, Chiefly in Southern-Africk*, in *A Collection of Voyages and Travels*, 4 vols., trans. and ed. Awnsham Churchill and John Churchill (London: Printed for A. & J. Churchill, 1704), vol. 1, pp. 673, 690, 693 (quotations). See also A. J. Gurevich, "Time as a Problem of Cultural History," in *Cultures and Time*, ed. Louis Gardet et al. (Paris: UNESCO, 1976), pp. 229–45; and Geertz, "Person, Time, and Conduct in Bali."

14. Thornton, *Kongolese Saint Anthony*, chap. 5 (quotations on pp. 113–14, 115). Thornton's translation of this prayer was made directly from the Kikongo version into English; see p. 115, n.4.

15. Ibid., pp. 117 (quotation), 118, 159–60, 184, 187. See also Hilton, *Kingdom of Kongo*, pp. 92–93.

16. Hilton, *Kingdom of Kongo*, pp. 207 (first quotation), 92 (second quotation). See also Thornton, *Kongolese Saint Anthony*, pp. 119, 157. On Mary's image in the Kongo and surrounding regions, see Merolla da Sorrento, *Voyage to Congo*, p. 716.

17. Hilton, *Kingdom of Kongo*, pp. 96–103 (quotation on p. 102).

18. Thornton, *Kongolese Saint Anthony*, pp. 160 (first quotation), 114; Filippo Pigafetta, *A Report of the Kingdom of Congo, and of the Surrounding Countries; Drawn out of the Writings and Discourses of the Portuguese, Duarte Lopez*, trans. and ed. Margarite Hutchinson (1881; repr., New York, 1970), pp. 84–85 (second quotation on p. 85); Thornton, "'I Am the Subject of the King of Congo': African Political Ideology and the Haitian Revolution," *Journal of World History* 4 (Fall 1993): 181–214 (third quotation on p. 188).

19. Olwell, *Masters, Slaves, and Subjects*, pp. 51–52.

20. Hilton, *Kingdom of Kongo*, p. 102. The Virgin's nativity was a date recorded even in Protestant calendars of eighteenth-century North America. See *Job Shepherd, Poor Job. 1752: An Almanack for the Year of Our Lord 1752*, in the Jacob Cushing Diaries, 1749–1809, Peter Force Collection, ser. 8D, microfilm, reel 36, p. 30 (Manuscript Division, Library of Congress, Washington, D.C.), which lists the "Nativity of Virgin Mary" as a significant date. Of course, it was

celebrated on September 8 ordinarily, although in 1752 it was observed on September 19 for that year only. The nativity was recorded in later almanacs, too. See the entry for September 8 ("Nat. B.V. Mary") in *Palladium of Knowledge: or, the Carolina and Georgia Almanac for the Year of Our Lord, 1798, and 11–23 of American Independence* (Charleston: Young, 1798), n.p. On the celebration in 1565 in Spanish Florida, see R. K. Sewall, *Sketches of St. Augustine* (1848; repr., Gainesville: University Presses of Florida, 1976), p. 18. For remarks on the importance of the feast of Mary's nativity to the Catholic faith historically, see Marina Warner, *Alone of All Her Sex: The Myth and the Cult of the Virgin Mary* (New York: Knopf, 1976), pp. 66–67, 106.

21. Merolla da Sorrento, *Voyage to Congo*, p. 693.

22. Haitians, notes Leslie G. Desmangles, also observe Marian dates, although some are apparently unsure why. She describes a *symbiosis by identity*, a process whereby "Elizi, the beautiful water goddess of love in Vodou, whose originals exist . . . in the African goddess of the same name in Whydah in Dahomey . . . becomes the Virgin Mary" and concludes that "although Vodouisants do not know the actual significance of Assumption Day (except that it is dedicated to Mary), Vodou ceremonies are held in Elizi's honor on that day"; Desmangles, *The Faces of the Gods: Vodou and Roman Catholicism in Haiti* (Chapel Hill: University of Chapel Hill Press, 1992), pp. 10 (first and second quotations), 144 (third quotation).

23. George P. Rawick, ed., *The American Slave: A Composite Autobiography: Supplement, Series 1*, vol. 11, *North Carolina and South Carolina Narratives* (Westport, Conn.: Greenwood, 1977), pp. 98–99 (first quotation), 100 (second quotation); Thornton, "African Dimensions," pp. 1106–8; Wood, *Black Majority*, pp. 313–14.

24. Edmund Quincy, "Mount Verney: Or, an Incident of Insurrection," *Liberty Bell* (Boston) (1847; repr. in *American Periodical Series*, II, reel 491), pp. 165–228, 193–95 (on Arnold's literacy), 216 (first quotation), 211 (second quotation), 215 (third quotation), 216–17 (fifth quotation), 219 (on the encounter with Bull); Wood, *Black Majority*, p. 315 (fourth quotation). See also Edgar, *South Carolina: A History* (Columbia: University of South Carolina Press, 1998), pp. 74–78; and Littlefield, *Rice and Slaves*, p. 17.

25. See, for example, Thornton, "African Dimensions." On masculinity, see Edward A. Pearson, "'A Countryside Full of Flames': A Reconsideration of the Stono Rebellion and Slave Rebelliousness in the Early Eighteenth-Century South Carolina Lowcountry," *Slavery and Abolition* 17 (August 1996): 22–50.

26. Thornton, "African Dimensions," p. 1111, n. 65; Wood, *Black Majority*, p. 316, n. 30. Wood relies on the general analysis offered by William C. Suttles Jr., "African Religious Survivals as Factors in American Slave Revolts," *Journal of Negro History* 56 (April 1971): 97–104, who does not address the Stono Rebellion. More recently, Olwell makes the rather literal connection between a contemporary's remark that the slaves marched "with Colours displayed" and Olaudah Equiano's recollection "that when our people march to the field [of battle], a red flag or banner is born before them." The "Colours" noted by the contemporary probably meant "colors" in the military sense—a flag or ensign that is not necessarily colored. Quoted in Olwell, *Masters, Slaves, and Subjects*, p. 22 (text and n. 12).

27. Thornton, *Kongolese Saint Anthony*, pp. 26–27 (quotation on p. 27). On the cathedral see *A Curious and Exact Account of a Voyage to Congo, In the Years 1666, and 1667. By the R.R.F.F. Michael Angelo of Gattina, and Denis de Carli of Piacenza, Capuchins, and Apostolick Missioners into the Said Kingdom of Kongo*, in *Collection of Voyages*, ed. Churchill and Churchill, vol. 1, p. 621.

Michael Gomez agrees with Hilton's argument that the "*nkadi mpemba*" was a "white-colored realm associated with death and the grave" but elaborates: "Now, the thing about *mpemba* is that it was located beneath the ground, 'on the other side of the water,' where white clay is found (that is, at the bottom of rivers and lakes)." Whiteness, he maintains, was associated with white people (who came from the other side of the water—the Atlantic), the slave trade, and death. They were "all inextricably linked" in Kongolese cosmology. Perhaps, then, the Stono rebels gathered near the Stono River (a body of water) for spiritual as well as logistical reasons. Michael Gomez, *Exchanging Our Country Marks: The Transformation of African Identities in the Colonial and Antebellum South* (Chapel Hill: University of North Carolina Press, 1998), pp. 146–47.

28. Rawick, *American Slave: Supplement, Ser. I*, vol. 11, p. 100 (quotation).

29. Thornton, "African Dimensions," pp. 1102–3, 1111–12; Olwell, *Masters, Slaves, and Subjects*, pp. 22–23; Morgan, *Slave Counterpoint*, p. 455; Berlin, *Many Thousands Gone*, pp. 73–74.

30. Merolla da Sorrento, *Voyage to Congo*, p. 622 (first quotation); Thornton, *Kongolese Saint Anthony*, p. 213 (second quotation). Mary as protector and warrior is a common image, and she can be found "putting in a judicious appearance to hearten her champions" at least since the seventh century; Warner, *Alone of All Her Sex*, pp. 304 (quotation), 305, 308, 313–14. See also Kevin Gosner, *Soldiers of the Virgin: The Moral Economy of a Colonial Maya Rebellion* (Tucson: University of Arizona Press, 1992); and Jaroslav Pelikan, *Mary through the Centuries: Her Place in the History of Culture* (New Haven: Yale University Press, 1996). On the prepolitical and political nature of slave resistance generally, see Eugene D. Genovese, *From Rebellion to Revolution: Afro-American Slave Revolts in the Making of the Modern World* (Baton Rouge: Louisiana State University Press, 1979); on the political implications of the Stono Rebellion in particular, consult Landers, *Black Society*, p. 34.

31. See, for example, the travel journal of David Peterson DeVries, who came from Holland accustomed to the new-style calendar but, following a brief stint in old-style Virginia, became confused as to the actual date. See Mark M. Smith, "Culture, Commerce, and Calendar Reform in Colonial America," *William and Mary Quarterly* 3rd ser., 55 (October 1998): 557–84, esp. 576, n. 53.

32. Desmangles makes a similar point in her excellent discussion of vodou and Catholicism in Haiti, where she notes: "The gods of Africa are related to calendrical events and are identified with natural phenomena. . . . Under the intense missionary activity that accompanied slavery in colonial Haiti, the African priests transported as slaves to Saint-Domingue were torn between two irreconcilable chronological systems—the Christian cycle of holy days, and the recurring cycle of mythical deeds performed *ab origine* in honor of their African deities. . . . This meant that they had to adapt their traditional calendar to the Gregorian calendar. . . . [T]he slaves in Saint-Domingue took the major Catholic feast days to perform their African ceremonies." Because Kongolese slaves were already calendrically Catholicized, they had less adjustment to make; Desmangles, *Faces of the Gods*, p. 10.

33. See, for example, Barbara Adam, *Timewatch: The Social Analysis of Time* (Cambridge: Polity Press / Cambridge, Mass.: Blackwell, 1995).

34. William Warren, "The Capture of Fort Michilimackinac," in *Cry of the Thunderbird: The American Indian's Own Story*, ed. Charles Hamilton (1950; repr., Norman: University of Oklahoma Press, 1972), p. 135. For some recent thoughts on time, race, and the temporal

consciousness of peoples of the African Diaspora, see Smith, "Questioning Colored Peoples' Time: The Importance of Punctuality for Black Resistance in the American South, 1739 and 1955," unpublished paper presented at a conference entitled "On Time: History, Science, Commemoration," at the National Museums and Galleries on Merseyside, Liverpool, England, September 16–19, 1999; Walter Johnson, "Possible Pasts: Some Speculations on Time, Temporality, and Atlantic Slavery," *Amerikastudien/American Studies* 45, no. 4 (2000): 485–99; and Kevin K. Birth, *"Any Time Is Trinidad Time": Social Meanings and Temporal Consciousness* (Gainesville: University Presses of Florida, 1999).

35. Berlin, *Many Thousands Gone*, esp. pp. 73–74.

# A WORKING BIBLIOGRAPHY
## ON THE STONO REBELLION

Below is a convenient and reasonably thorough compilation of primary and secondary sources relevant to an understanding of the Stono Rebellion. Some of these sources are noted in the editor's introduction, the scholarly essays, and in the documents. I have not noted every secondary work that simply mentions the Stono Rebellion. Instead, I have listed works offering detail concerning the revolt or that aid our understanding of the context in which the revolt occurred.

### Primary

These sources are listed in chronological order, beginning with the earliest.

"The Journal of William Stephens." In *The Colonial Records of the State of Georgia*. Vol. 4, *Stephens' Journal 1737–1740*, edited by Allen D. Candler, pp. 378–79, 412–13. Atlanta: Franklin, 1906.

"Letters from Charlestown in South Carolina, of the 14th of September," *Boston Gazette*, October 29–November 5, 1739.

"A Ranger's Report of Travels with General Oglethorpe, 1739–1742." In *Travels in the American Colonies*, edited by Newton D. Mereness, pp. 222–23. New York: Macmillan, 1916.

Robert Pringle, Charles Town, to John Richards, London, 26 September, 1739. In *The Letterbook of Robert Pringle*. Vol. 1, *April 2, 1737–September 25, 1742*, edited by Walter B. Edgar, pp. 134–35. Columbia: University of South Carolina Press, 1972.

Diary entry, Friday, September 28, 1739. In *Detailed Reports on the Salzberger Emigrants Who Settled in America . . . Edited by Samuel Urlsperger*. Vol. 6, *1739*, translated and edited by George Fenwick Jones and Renate Wilson, p. 226. Athens: University of Georgia Press, 1981.

"A Letter from South Carolina [September 28, 1739]," *Boston Weekly News-Letter*, November 1–8, 1739.

"Extract of a Letter from S. Carolina, dated October 2," *Gentleman's Magazine* 10 (March 1740): 127–29.

"Account of the Negroe Insurrection in South Carolina." In *The Colonial Records of the State of Georgia*, edited by Allen D. Candler, Wm. L. Northern, and Lucian L. Knight, vol. 22, prt. 2, pp. 232–36. Atlanta: Byrd, 1913.

Lt. Gov. Sir William Bull to the Board of Trade, Charleston, October 5, 1739, (Received December 10, 1739), Sainsbury Transcripts, Records in the British Public Record Office Relating to South Carolina, 1711–1782, vol. 20, pp. 179–80. C.O. Papers, S.C. Original Correspondence, Secretary of State, 1730–1746, no. 5/388), South Carolina Department of Archives and History (hereinafter SCDAH), Columbia.

A Commons House of Assembly Committee Report, in a Message to the Governor's Council, *Journal of the Upper House*, no. 7 (November 29, 1739), pp. 266–67, SCDAH.

Andrew Leslie to the Society for the Propagation of the Gospel, 7 January 1739/40, Society for the Propagation of the Gospel Record, microfilm, reel 5, pp. 19–20, SCDAH.

"Act for the better ordering and governing of Negroes and other Slaves in this Province," May, 1740. In *The Statutes at Large of South Carolina*, edited by Thomas Cooper and David J. McCord, vol. 7, pp. 397–417. Columbia, S.C.: Johnston, 1840.

"Report of the Committee Appointed to Enquire into the Causes of the Disappointment of Success in the Late Expedition Against St. Augustine." In *Journal of the Commons House of Assembly*, edited by J. H. Easterby et al. Columbia, S.C., 1953, 1 July 1741, pp. 83–84.

Hewatt, Alexander. *An Historical Account of the Rise and Progress of the Colonies of South Carolina and Georgia*, 2 vols. (London, 1779). Reprinted in *Historical Collections of South Carolina; Embracing Many Rare and Valuable Pamphlets, and Other Documents, Relating to the History of That State, from Its First Discovery to Its Independence, in the Year 1776*, edited by B. R. Carroll, vol. 1, pp. 331–33. New York, 1836.

"Governor William Bull's Representation of the Colony, 1770." In *The Colonial South Carolina Scene: Contemporary Views, 1697–1774*, edited by H. Roy Merrens, p. 260. Columbia, S.C., 1977.

Quincy, Edmund. "Mount Verney: Or, an Incident of Insurrection." *Liberty Bell* (Boston) (1847): 165–228.

Rawick, George P., ed. *The American Slave: A Composite Autobiography: Supplement, Series 1.* Vol. 11, *North Carolina and South Carolina Narratives*, pp. 98–100. Westport, Conn.: Greenwood, 1977.

### Secondary

Berlin, Ira. *Many Thousands Gone: The First Two Centuries of Slavery in North America.* Cambridge, Mass.: Belknap Press of Harvard University Press, 1998.

Burris, Roddie. "Failed Uprising Resulted in Harsher Life for Slaves." *Columbia State*, Sunday, February 2, 2003, p. B1, 6.

Carney, Judith. *Black Rice: The African Origins of Rice Cultivation in the Americas.* Cambridge, Mass.: Harvard University Press, 2002.

Chaplin, Joyce E. *An Anxious Pursuit: Agricultural Innovation and Modernity in the Lower South, 1730–1815.* Chapel Hill: University of North Carolina Press, 1993.

Coclanis, Peter A. *The Shadow of a Dream: Economic Life and Death in the South Carolina Low Country, 1670–1920.* New York: Oxford University Press, 1989.

Creel, Margaret Washington. *A Peculiar People: Slave Religion and Community-Culture among the Gullahs.* New York: New York University Press, 1988.

Edgar, Walter. *South Carolina: A History.* Columbia: University of South Carolina Press, 1998.

Farley, M. Foster. "A History of Negro Slave Revolts in South Carolina." *Afro-American Studies* 3 (1972): 97–102.

Fox-Genovese, Elizabeth. "Strategies and Forms of Resistance: Focus on Slave Women in the United States." In *In Resistance: Studies in African, Caribbean, and Afro-American History,* edited by Gary Y. Okihiro, pp. 143–65. Amherst: University of Massachusetts Press, 1986.

Gomez, Michael. *Exchanging Our Country Marks: The Transformation of African Identity in the Colonial and Antebellum South.* Chapel Hill: University of North Carolina Press, 1998.

Heuman, Gad, ed. *Out of the House of Bondage: Runaways, Resistance, and Marronage in Africa and the New World.* London: Cass, 1986.

Hoffer, Peter Charles. *Sensory Worlds in Early America.* Baltimore: Johns Hopkins University Press, 2003.

Johnson, Michael P. "Runaway Slaves and the Slave Communities in South Carolina, 1799 to 1830." *William and Mary Quarterly* 3rd ser., 38 (July 1981): 418–41.

Kay, Marvin L. Michael, and Lorin Lee Cary. "'They Are Indeed the Constant Plague of Their Tyrants': Slave Defence of a Moral Economy in Colonial North Carolina, 1748–1772." In *Out of the House of Bondage: Runaways, Resistance, and Marronage in Africa and the New World,* edited by Gad Heuman, pp. 37–56. London: Cass, 1986.

Klingberg, Frank J. *An Appraisal of the Negro in Colonial South Carolina: A Study in Americanization.* Washington, D.C.: Associated Publishers, 1941.

Laing, Annette. "'Heathens and Infidels'? African Christianization and Anglicanism in the South Carolina Low Country, 1700–1750." *Religion and American Culture* 12 (Summer 2002): 197–228.

Landers, Jane. *Black Society in Spanish Florida.* Urbana: University of Illinois Press, 1999.

———. "Gracia Real de Santa Teresa de Mose: A Free Black Town in Spanish Colonial Florida." *American Historical Review* 95 (February 1990): 9–30.

Linebaugh, Peter, and Marcus Rediker. *The Many-Headed Hydra: Sailors, Slaves, Commoners, and the Hidden History of the Revolutionary Atlantic.* Boston: Beacon, 2000.

Littlefield, Daniel C. *Rice and Slaves: Ethnicity and the Slave Trade in Colonial South Carolina.* Baton Rouge: Louisiana State University Press, 1981.

McCrady, Edward. *The History of South Carolina under the Royal Government, 1719–1776.* New York: Macmillan, 1901.

Meaders, Daniel E. "South Carolina Fugitives as Viewed through Local Colonial Newspapers with Emphasis on Runaway Notices, 1732–1801." *Journal of Negro History* 60 (April 1975): 288–319.

Moore, John Alexander. "Royalizing South Carolina: The Revolution of 1719 and the Evolution of Early South Carolina Government." Ph.D. diss., University of South Carolina, 1991.

Morgan, Philip D. "Colonial South Carolina Runaways: Their Significance for Slave Culture." In *Out of the House of Bondage: Runaways, Resistance, and Marronage in Africa and the New World,* edited by Gad Heuman, pp. 57–78. London: Cass, 1986.

———. *Slave Counterpoint: Black Culture in the Eighteenth-Century Chesapeake and Lowcountry.* Chapel Hill: University of North Carolina Press, 1998.

Mullin, Michael. *Africa in America: Slave Acculturation and Resistance in the American South and the British Caribbean, 1736–1831.* Urbana: University of Illinois Press, 1992.

———, ed. *American Negro Slavery: A Documentary History.* Columbia: University of South Carolina Press, 1976.

Okihiro, Gary Y., ed. *In Resistance: Studies in African, Caribbean, and Afro-American History.* Amherst: University of Massachusetts Press, 1986.

Olwell, Robert. *Masters, Slaves, and Subjects: The Culture of Power in the South Carolina Low Country, 1740–1790*. Ithaca, N.Y.: Cornell University Press, 1998.

Patterson, Orlando. *Slavery and Social Death: A Comparative Study*. Cambridge, Mass.: Harvard University Press, 1982.

Pearson, Edward A. "'A Countryside Full of Flames': A Reconsideration of the Stono Rebellion and Slave Rebelliousness in the Early Eighteenth-Century South Carolina Lowcountry." *Slavery and Abolition* 17, no. 2 (1996): 22–50.

Phillips, U. B. *American Negro Slavery*. New York and London: Appleton, 1918.

Rath, Richard Cullen. "Drums and Power: Ways of Creolizing Music in Coastal South Carolina and Georgia, 1730–90." In *Creolization in the Americas*, edited by David Buisseret and Steven G. Reinhardt, pp. 99–130. College Station: Texas A&M Press, 2000.

———. *How Early America Sounded*. Ithaca, N.Y.: Cornell University Press, 2003.

Richardson, David. "The British Slave Trade to Colonial South Carolina." *Slavery and Abolition* 12 (December 1991): 125–72.

Shick, Tom W. "Healing and Race in the South Carolina Low Country." In *Africans in Bondage: Studies in Slavery and the Slave Trade*, edited by Paul Lovejoy, pp. 107–24. Madison: University of Wisconsin Press, 1986.

Sirmans, M. Eugene. *Colonial South Carolina: A Political History, 1663–1763*. Chapel Hill: University of North Carolina Press, 1966.

Smith, Henry A. M. "Willtown or New London." *South Carolina Historical and Genealogical Magazine* 10 (January 1909): 20–32.

Smith, Mark M. "Remembering Mary, Shaping Revolt: Reconsidering the Stono Rebellion." *Journal of Southern History* 67 (August 2001): 513–34.

Suttles, William C., Jr. "African Religious Survivals as Factors in American Slave Revolts." *Journal of Negro History* 56 (April 1971): 97–104.

TePaske, John J. "The Fugitive Slave: Intercolonial Rivalry and Spanish Slave Policy, 1687–1764." In *Eighteenth-Century Florida and Its Borderlands*, edited by Samuel Proctor, pp. 1–12. Gainesville: University Presses of Florida, 1975.

Thornton, John K. "Dimensions of the Stono Rebellion." *American Historical Review* 96 (October 1991): 1101–13.

———. *The Kongolese Saint Anthony: Dona Beatriz Kimpa Vita and the Antonian Movement, 1684–1706*. Cambridge and New York: Cambridge University Press, 1998.

Wax, Darold D. "'The Great Risque We Run': The Aftermath of Slave Rebellion at Stono, South Carolina, 1739–1745." *Journal of Negro History* 67 (Summer 1982): 136–47.

Weir, Robert M. *Colonial South Carolina: A History*. Millwood, N.Y.: KTO, 1983.

Wish, Harvey. "American Slave Insurrections before 1861." *Journal of Negro History* 22 (July 1937): 299–320.

Wood, Peter H. *Black Majority: Negroes in Colonial South Carolina from 1670 through the Stono Rebellion*. New York: Knopf, 1974.

# INDEX